A Casebook for Exploring Diversity

A Casebook for Exploring Diversity

THIRD EDITION

George L. Redman
Hamline University

Upper Saddle River, New Jersey
Columbus, Ohio

Library of Congress Cataloging-in-Publication Data

Redman, George.

A casebook for exploring diversity / George L. Redman.—3rd ed.

p. cm.

Includes bibliographical references.

ISBN 0-13-170806-6

1. Multicultural education—United States. 2. Pluralism (Social sciences)—United States. 3. Case method. 4. Teachers—Training of—United States. I. Title.

LC1099.3.P43 2007

370.117—dc22   2005029499

Vice President and Executive Publisher: Jeffery W. Johnston
Executive Editor: Debra A. Stollenwerk
Senior Editorial Assistant: Mary Morrill
Assistant Development Editor: Elisa Rogers
Production Editor: Kris Roach
Production Coordination: Carlisle Editorial Services
Design Coordinator: Diane C. Lorenzo
Photo Coordinator: Monica Merkel
Cover Designer: Aaron Dixon
Cover Image: Corbis
Production Manager: Susan Hannahs
Director of Marketing: David Gesell
Senior Marketing Manager: Darcy Betts Prybella
Marketing Coordinator: Brian Mounts

This book was set in Times by Carlisle Publishing Services. It was printed and bound by R.R. Donnelley & Sons Company. The cover was printed by R.R. Donnelley & Sons Company.

Photo Credits: Barbara Schwartz/Merrill, pp. 1, 125; Prentice Hall School Division, p. 9; David Mager/Pearson Learning Photo Studio, p. 27; Charles Gatewood/PH College, p. 43; George Dodson/PH College, p. 67; Elliot Smith/Silver Burdett Ginn, p. 83; Scott Cunningham/Merrill, p. 97; Ken Karp/PH College, p. 111; Laima Druskis/PH College, p. 141.

Pearson Education Ltd.
Pearson Education Singapore Pte. Ltd.
Pearson Education Canada, Ltd.
Pearson Education—Japan

Pearson Education Australia Pty. Limited
Pearson Education North Asia Ltd.
Pearson Educación de Mexico, S.A. de C.V.
Pearson Education Malaysia Pte. Ltd.

10 9 8 7 6 5 4

ISBN: 0-13-170806-6

PREFACE

Book Organization

The third edition of *A Casebook for Exploring Diversity* presents 37 case examples of realistic classroom events, situations, and issues for analysis and inquiry, focusing on the topics of gender, ethnicity, race, socioeconomic status, religion, special needs, sexual orientation, language, and ageism.

This casebook is a text supplement for use in courses on multicultural/inclusive/urban education, as well as in foundations and methods courses in which course or program goals reflect concern for cultural diversity. It is also a useful resource in professional development programs designed to stimulate reflection and action in schools in increasingly diverse societies.

It is assumed that your primary course text will introduce, provide the theoretical and/or research base for, and show relationships among basic terms and concepts such as:

prejudice	classism
stereotype	self-esteem
discrimination	sexism
oppression	ethnicity
racism	culture
multicultural curriculum	power

To assist in identifying common definitions for key terms, a glossary of selected terms is provided at the back of this text.

As a text supplement, this casebook provides (1) illustrations or examples of real classroom events, (2) problems for analysis and inquiry, and/or (3) frames for developing storied knowledge of teaching. The cases herein can create in students a need to know about concepts and/or extend thinking about such concepts. The questions at the end of each case encourage the reader to think about diversity issues as well as teaching methods, student learning, child or adolescent needs, and moral aspects of teaching.

The case analysis approach in this text is consistent with the trend toward constructivism in teacher education, in which teachers are invited to become active inquirers in their work in schools, and in so doing to emphasize reflectivity, interaction, speculative thinking, contextual influence, and personal meaning making.

The stories in this collection represent real classroom situations. Their generic nature makes them relevant to teachers and prospective teachers in grades pre-K to 12 and throughout the full range of subject matter areas. Each case contains at least one cultural diversity issue, as well as other issues related to teaching and learning.

Features

This casebook has several characteristic features.

Provides Focused Cases

First, while the cases offer opportunities for analysis on more than one level and are sufficiently complex to invite multiple interpretations, they are also more focused than many cases. Hence, instructors will find that they can be used more flexibly.

Stimulates Thinking at Various Levels

"Questions for Reflection" invite students to collect further data, consider alternative perspectives, share their thoughts with others, and formulate individual or group responses.

"Activities for Extending Thinking" encourage students to think about cause-and-effect relationships; develop and use categories of knowledge, skills, and dispositions; and build and evaluate new paradigms and models. Students are invited to relate insights to the course text, to field experiences, to the lesson and unit planning process, and to local, state, and national standards in teacher education.

Some of the questions and activities encourage students to deepen and broaden their understanding of diversity issues by investigating resources beyond those listed in this casebook, e.g., local or regional advocacy agencies in their own geographical area.

Provides Resources for Connecting to the Knowledge Base

Extensive references and resources are offered as a bridge to the knowledge base. Selected readings and Internet resources related to each of the 10 diversity domains are provided at the end of each chapter. In addition, a list of relevant general sources is provided in the resources at the end of the book.

Provides Opportunities for Students to Become Actively Involved in Case Design

This book provides the opportunity for readers to help construct the context in which they will analyze a given case, as well as to design cases of their own. Individuals or small groups in a course or workshop can consider a given case within more than one context. Doing so serves to highlight the importance of contextual conditions that affect teaching and learning. Suggestions for adding context are provided in Resource A. Furthermore, to encourage active involvement in their own learning, students are invited to construct a case of their own at the end of each chapter.

Provides Cases Representing Interpersonal Competence and Multicultural Content

Each case herein falls under one or both of the classifications *interpersonal competence* or *multicultural content*. As a guide for both students and instructors, the matrix in Resource D places each case into the categories of interpersonal competence (cases that focus on personal skills that demonstrate cultural sensitivity) and/or multicultural content (cases that illustrate the use of multicultural curriculum in a subject matter context).

Consistent with characteristics of cases suggested by Fauske (2000), the cases in this casebook:

■ have shorter vignettes
■ allow focus on one or more than one objective
■ encourage divergent responses initially, followed by a tentative decision on the preferred way to address the key issue in the case
■ allow student initiation of analysis, followed by instructor guidance in the form of questions for reflection
■ allow flexibility for amount of instructor direction, e.g., relating of case to students' prior experience, curriculum development, current clinical experience, professional standards, or an outcome determined by the instructor to be critical
■ provide resources for further exploration of issues in the case

New to This Edition

■ *Glossary.* A glossary of key terms has been added to assist in discussing issues embedded in the cases.
■ *Ageism.* A new chapter consisting of cases related to ageism has been added.
■ *New Cases.* New cases have been added in the following areas: gender, religion, sexual orientation, and language. In addition, new "Questions for Reflection" allow exploration of new topics within cases, including profanity, mental health issues such as anxiety and depression, sexually explicit dress, responses to terrorism, and immigrant and refugee status.
■ *Bibliography of Multicultural Children's Literature.* Resource E contains multicultural children's literature for pre-K–12 teachers' use with elementary and secondary students. It is provided to aid preservice and in-service teachers completing "Questions for Reflection" and "Activities for Extending Thinking" that require the development of curriculum related to a given case. It is also helpful to those wanting to enjoy and learn about stories from other cultures. Resource E is divided into two parts. Part I: Print Resources contains picture books representing the following cultures: Afghani, African, Asian, Bosnian, Cambodian, Chinese, Indian, Islam/Muslim, Japanese, Jewish-American, Korean, Native American people, Palestinian, Phillippine, Thai, Tibetan, and Vietnamese. It also includes books representing persons of multiracial backgrounds,

the area of race relations, and reviews, guides, and curriculum resources. Chapter books include resources on a variety of cultures. Part II: Internet Resources includes sites on children's literature in general, advocacy and educational equity, African-American, Native-American, and Latino cultures, and resources on women and girls.

- *Rubrics.* Rubrics for assessment of student responses to cases are included in Resource F.
- *Retention and Updates of Best Cases.* Based on analysis of ratings of over 200 students in an urban-based preservice teacher education program, only the highest-rated cases have been preserved in each part.
- *Broader View of Institutional Level.* While the primary focus of the diversity cases is on the individual teacher and his/her classroom, some "Questions for Reflection" and "Activities for Extending Thinking" that help to focus on broader institutional policies and practices within the school and community have been added.
- *Clinical Experiences/Curriculum Development.* Similarly, a number of "Questions for Reflection" and "Activities for Extending Thinking" that relate the cases to local, state, and national standards, to clinical experiences, and to curriculum development have been added.
- *Updated Print and Internet Resources.* The most recent print and Internet resources reflect the most current research and best practice in the profession.

Format

Chapter 1 provides an introduction to the text, with a brief discussion of the benefits of case methodology and a description of the cases in this text, as well as the process for analyzing and discussing the cases and for pursuing follow-up activities. Chapters 2 through 10 provide cases representing key areas of cultural diversity in education. Each case follows this format:

- Begins with a brief overview of the story
- Provides a concise story illustrating at least one diversity issue (some cases also provide the opportunity for analysis of pedagogical issues)
- Offers "Questions for Reflection" and "Activities for Extending Thinking"

At the end of each chapter, students are invited to construct a case of their own. Finally, a bibliography and a listing of selected Internet sites that relate to the diversity area of that section are provided.

Resources

Resource A includes guidelines for creating additional context for a given case, a table illustrating proportions of ethnic groups represented in the U.S. population, and projections of the number of students who would comprise a "typical" classroom based on those projections. **Resource B** offers a model illustrating four levels of integration of multicultural curriculum (Banks, 2005). **Resource C** provides a form to use in designing your own cases.

Resource D provides a matrix that identifies each case as either *interpersonal competence* or *multicultural content* or both. **Resource E** provides a bibliography of multicultural children's literature. **Resource F** offers rubrics for self, peer, and instructor assessment of student responses to cases.

Acknowledgments

For their ongoing love and support, not only in the writing of this casebook, but in all my efforts, I thank my family members: Shari, Ryan, and Angie. Each truly has been a blessing in my life.

In acknowledging others who contributed to the book, I begin by thanking Dr. Eugene Anderson, professor of education (retired), University of Minnesota. His mentorship in ways of thinking about education and teacher education has been invaluable. I have valued deeply his friendship, guidance, and support over the years. His suggestions regarding the organization and overall readability of this book have been most appreciated.

For her analysis of case-study format, validity, and integrity of concepts and her multicultural sensitivity, I thank Darcia Narvaez, Department of Curriculum and Instruction, University of Minnesota. Her work significantly strengthened the conceptual and theoretical aspects of the book.

I thank the many pre-K-to-12 teachers and undergraduate and graduate students in teacher education who reviewed the cases. Their assessment of the degree of clarity and realism of each of the cases helped greatly in confirming their potential for wider use. In particular, I thank Bonnie Houseman, English as a Second Language (ESL) teacher candidate; Jon Halpern and Jeff Fink, veteran elementary teachers; Ann Mabbott, director of Second Language Teaching and Learning at Hamline University; Sam Hernandez, veteran secondary teacher; and Deborah L. Harris, parent, for their valuable reviews.

I thank Dr. Charles Bruning, professor of education, close friend and mentor. His wise counsel regarding the content of this book and his positive spirit over the years have been encouraging indeed.

Debbie Stollenwerk, executive editor, Merrill/Prentice Hall; Mary Morrill, senior editorial assistant, Merrill/Prentice Hall; Elisa Rogers, assistant development editor Merrill/Prentice Hall; and Mary Tindle, Carlisle Editorial Services, have done a superb job in establishing a comfortable working relationship for creating and writing. I appreciate the guidance they have so generously provided.

David Albornoz, Christopher Swanson, and Simon Gandica, all of Hamline University, helped in the preparation of the manuscript. I thank Julie Johnson for her work on the bibliography of multicultural children's literature.

I am also grateful to the following reviewers: Paul C. Gorski, Hamline University; Nancy L. Hadaway, University of Texas at Arlington; Nadine Haley, Metropolitan State University; JoAnn Hohenbrink, Ohio Dominican University; Kimberlye P. Joyce, University of Richmond; Theresa M. Richardson, Ball State University; and Kevin S. Thrasher, Grand Canyon University.

I thank two persons who have had direct involvement in the development of portions of this edition of this casebook. First, I thank Dr. Dwight C. Watson, for his encouragement and support on the development of cases related to race and ethnicity, especially the case designed to help with the deconstruction of the "N" word (Case 13), the context for the case on oppression and whiteness (Case 15), and on the development of the assessment rubrics in Resource F. As a colleague and close friend, he has generously shared his expertise in various areas within multicultural education, as well as in the areas of reading and literacy, and curriculum and instruction. His many contributions have indeed enriched this edition of this casebook.

The second person with ideas leading directly to the development of a number of the cases in this edition is Angela Redman, a veteran teacher in both regular and special education and an experienced school administrator. Her translation of real incidents from recent classroom and school experience in the Phoenix area schools has contributed significantly to the revision of current cases, especially those related to gender, GLBT issues, and exceptionality, as well as to the development of a new section (Chapter 10) on ageism. Her editing of current cases, sharing of experiences that lead to the creation of new cases, and actual writing of stories on which additional new cases were based have added important new dimensions to this edition.

Last, without the encouragement and support of my colleagues at Hamline University, completion of this casebook would not have been possible. I extend sincere thanks to each of the following members of the Education Department: Colleen Bell, Jim Bonilla, Nancy Desmond, Steve Jongewaard, Therese Kiley, Lenore Kinne, Kim Koeppen, Kristy Okerlund, Jean Strait, Dwight Watson, and Joy Wimsatt, as well as to the college faculty as a whole.

References

Banks, J. A. (2001). Approaches to multicultural curriculum reform. In J. A. Banks and C. A. M. Banks (Eds.), *Multicultural education: Issues and perspectives* (4th ed., pp. 225–246). New York: Wiley.

Fauske, J. R. (2000). Linguistic and instructional precision in teaching with cases and problems. *Journal of Cases in Educational Leadership, 3*(2), feature essay.

Redman, G. L. (1999). *Teaching in today's classrooms: Cases from elementary school.* Upper Saddle River, NJ: Merrill/Prentice Hall.

Redman, G. L. (1999). *Teaching in today's classrooms: Cases from middle and secondary school.* Upper Saddle River, NJ: Merrill/Prentice Hall.

ABOUT THE AUTHOR

George Redman taught in the public schools for 7 years, including 4 years in the Los Angeles area and 3 in an urban school in Minneapolis. He has also served as professor 30 years in the undergraduate teacher education program at Hamline University in St. Paul, Minnesota. He has taught in the Hamline Continuing Education for Teachers Program for more than 15 years, and has conducted numerous in-service professional development workshops and courses for teachers throughout the region.

Dr. Redman's primary undergraduate responsibility has been for three courses: Education and Cultural Diversity, a core course in the program; Teaching in the Secondary School, a general methods course; and Student Teaching. He has also taught courses entitled City as Classroom, Values Education, Theory to Practice K–8, Families, Schools, and Communities, and Self and Other. He has served as chair of the department for more than 10 years. For each of the past 28 years he has supervised student teachers in urban schools in the Minneapolis/St. Paul metropolitan area.

Professor Redman is a recipient of the Association of Teacher Educators (ATE) national award for outstanding research, and he has published numerous articles in professional journals. His other books include *Teaching in Today's Classrooms: Cases from Elementary School, Teaching in Today's Classrooms: Cases from Middle and Secondary School, Building Self-Esteem in Students: A Skill and Strategy Workbook for Teachers,* and *Building Self-Esteem in Children: A Skill and Strategy Workbook for Parents.* He is co-author of *Self-Esteem for Tots to Teens, more recently translated and published in Japanese (1999) and Italian (2005).*

TEACHER PREP

**MERRILL
PRENTICE HALL**

Teacher Preparation Classroom

Your Class. Their Careers. Our Future. Will your students be prepared?

We invite you to explore our new, innovative and engaging website and all that it has to offer you, your course, and tomorrow's educators! Organized around the major courses pre-service teachers take, the Teacher Preparation site provides media, student/teacher artifacts, strategies, research articles, and other resources to equip your students with the quality tools needed to excel in their courses and prepare them for their first classroom.

This ultimate on-line education resource is available at no cost, when packaged with a Merrill text, and will provide you and your students access to:

Online Video Library. More than 150 video clips—each tied to a course topic and framed by learning goals and Praxis-type questions—capture real teachers and students working in real classrooms, as well as in-depth interviews with both students and educators.

Student and Teacher Artifacts. More than 200 student and teacher classroom artifacts—each tied to a course topic and framed by learning goals and application questions—provide a wealth of materials and experiences to help make your study to become a professional teacher more concrete and hands-on.

Research Articles. Over 500 articles from ASCD's renowned journal *Educational Leadership*. The site also includes Research Navigator, a searchable database of additional educational journals.

Teaching Strategies. Over 500 strategies and lesson plans for you to use when you become a practicing professional.

Licensure and Career Tools. Resources devoted to helping you pass your licensure exam; learn standards, law, and public policies; plan a teaching portfolio; and succeed in your first year of teaching.

CONTENTS

Note: Every effort has been made to provide accurate and current Internet information in this book. However, the Internet and information posted on it are constantly changing, so it is inevitable that some of the Internet addresses listed in this textbook will change.

Chapter 1

Introduction

Cases: What Are They?

Cases have been defined as engaging narrative stories containing events that unfold over a period of time in a specified place (Shulman, 1992). Within teacher education, such stories describe classroom or school-related events. They are stories of either real problems or hypothetical problems representing real ones and can be as short as a paragraph or as long as 50 pages. McNergney, Herbert, and Ford (1994, p. 340) assert that "good cases have possibilities for multiple levels of analysis and they are sufficiently complex to allow multiple interpretations."

The Cases in This Casebook

The cases in this collection describe events that occur in elementary, middle, and high school classrooms in urban, suburban, and rural settings. They represent dilemmas common to all classrooms, regardless of subject matter and grade level.

Each case focuses on at least one issue involving race, socioeconomic status, language, ethnicity, gender, sexual orientation, religion, disability, or age. In addition, each contains at least one issue related to planning, classroom environment, instruction, or professional responsibilities. Thus, each case can be used to stimulate thinking about diversity and/or pedagogical issues, depending on the orientation of a given course or workshop, and on the needs and interests of participants.

Multicultural Education

A definition of the term *culture* is basic to the understanding of multicultural education. Although the term can be defined in various ways, the broad definition offered by Pusch (1979) best serves the purpose of this text:

> Culture is the sum total of ways of living, including values, beliefs, aesthetic standards, linguistic expression, patterns of thinking, behavioral norms, and styles of communication which a group of people has developed to assure its survival in a particular physical and human environment. (p. 3)

Multiculturalism, then, invites teachers to integrate into their teaching information about the many cultures in their schools, communities, and the world. It has as its central goal the development in all students of an understanding of, and appreciation for, the human potential of persons of all backgrounds.

Carl Grant (1994, p. 4) defines multicultural education as a "philosophical concept and an educational process." As a philosophical concept, it is based on the ideals of "freedom, justice, equality, equity, and human dignity that are contained in United States documents such as the Constitution and the Declaration of Independence" (Grant, 1994, p. 4).

As an educational process, multicultural education informs all academic disciplines and other aspects of the curriculum. It prepares all students to work actively toward structural equality in the organizations and institutions of the United States. It helps students to develop positive self-concepts and to discover who they are, particularly in terms of their multiple group memberships. Multicultural education does this by providing knowledge about the history, culture, and contributions of the diverse groups that have shaped the history, politics, and culture of the United States. (Grant, 1994, p. 4)

It should be emphasized that multicultural content and intercultural competence should be integrated into all content areas rather than viewed as an "add-on" subject in itself.

Finally, Banks and Banks (2001, p. 20) identifies dimensions of multicultural education that can guide school reform: (1) integration of cultural content, (2) the knowledge construction process, (3) prejudice reduction, (4) an equity pedagogy, and (5) an empowering school culture and social structure.

The more that teachers examine, reflect on, and discuss these important dimensions, the more informed they will become and the more confident they will be when implementing them in classrooms and schools. The examination of authentic cases is one effective method for stimulating such reflection.

Cases and the Knowledge Base in Teacher Education

Case-based instruction is supported by the portion of the knowledge base that asserts that teachers' knowledge (1) is situation-specific (contextual), (2) is informed and informing through interaction (interactive), and (3) involves uncertainty (is speculative) (Clark & Lampert, 1986). Cases, then, provide situation-specific circumstances that can help students connect theory with practice in a supportive, interactive environment.

Schon (1987) observed that teachers acquire the bulk of their professional knowledge through continuous action and reflection on everyday problems. Case studies provide a common point of departure for reflecting on such problems and thus help teachers create meaning from complex teaching and learning situations.

A growing research base suggests varied benefits from reflecting on everyday problems. Through the analysis of authentic cases, teachers, businesspeople, lawyers, and others are said to develop the power to reason (Sprinthall & Theis-Sprinthall, 1983), enhance their cognitive complexity (Hunt & Sullivan, 1974; Oja & Sprinthall, 1978), perceive meaningfulness (Kennedy, 1991), alter their belief structure (Peterson, Carpenter, & Fennema, 1989), think like professionals (Kleinfeld, 1992; Morine-Dershimer, 1991), and develop other capacities through reflection. Although further research on case-method teaching is needed, interest is growing in its use to encourage the development of reflective action (McNergney, Herbert, & Ford, 1994).

Some scholars think of teacher reflection in terms of critical theory. McLaren (1989) viewed knowledge as determined by the surrounding culture, context, customs, and historical era. He observed that "critical pedagogy attempts to provide teachers . . . with a better means of understanding the role that schools actually play within a race-, class-, and gender-divided society" (p. 163).

Darling-Hammond (2000, p. 170) posits that "good teachers must develop an aware-ness of their own perspectives and how these can be enlarged to avoid a 'communicentric bias' (Gordon, 1990), which limits their understanding of those whom they teach." Case analysis in which multiple perspectives are explored can help expand one's communicen-tric bias. (For a review of this literature, see Darling-Hammond and Snyder, 1998.)

The Benefits of Case Studies

I've never taught in a school, urban or suburban, in which staff members freely discussed issues of race and class with one another. Racial tensions are almost always a factor among faculty, but they're almost never addressed. Because our society is so segregated, most of us don't discuss race in integrated settings, and schools don't provide opportunities for teachers—or students—to develop the skills and knowledge needed to examine "hot" is-sues, like race, with civility. (Weiner, 1999)

Cases provide an opportunity for both prospective and in-service teachers to anticipate real problems; to retrieve principles of teaching and learning to resolve those problems; and to construct, discuss, and evaluate responses in a community of learners. More specifically, according to Merseth (1991), as cited in Cooper (1995), case methods

1. help develop skills of critical analysis and problem solving, including skills of observing, making inferences, identifying relationships, and articulating organizing principles;
2. encourage reflective practice and deliberate action—they require students to discuss and choose from competing interpretations advanced by one another;
3. provide a context in which students can make decisions in complex situations when there is not an exact match between theory and practice;
4. involve students in their own learning—active responsibility takes the place of passive acceptance that might exist in a lecture situation; and
5. encourage the development of a community of learners by/through lively and engaging discussion and collaborative teamwork.

Creating Additional Context for the Cases

In Resource A, you will find an invitation to list community, school, and classroom factors that might make a case more rich, authentic, or personally relevant. You are invited to list fac-tors such as characteristics of the school and community (e.g., proportion of socioeconomic, ethnic, and religious groups) and the nature of the individuals and the classroom in the case (e.g., personal characteristics, type of curriculum). You may also find the information in Resource A on national estimates of various ethnic groups, children in poverty, exceptional-ity, and sexual orientation helpful.

Limit the number of details that you add to a given case—perhaps to four or five—so that the key issues in the case are not lost. Take a few minutes to list in writing the contextual details you will add. To further encourage your active participation in learning, your instructor may invite you to design a case study of your own. Directions for doing so are provided in Resource C.

Preparing and Participating in Discussions of Cases

The following steps are recommended to prepare for a case study discussion:

1. Read the case quickly for general understanding.
2. Consider adding cultural and educational context in which the case is set. Suggestions for doing so are offered in Resource A (see "Creating Additional Context for a Given Case").
3. Reread the case, taking notes on key issues and listing questions. Examine outside resources if time permits.
4. Complete the questions at the end of the case and any Activities for Extending Thinking assigned by your instructor.
5. Suggest ideas for activities that might extend thinking about the issue(s) in the case. For example, if you are aware of a resource or a site that could be visited by classmates to expand or refine thinking about an issue, suggest it to your instructor and your classmates.

Participation in class discussions of case studies should take place in the spirit of cooperation. Whether discussion occurs in large or small groups, your learning will be maximized if everyone has an equal opportunity to share ideas about an issue in the case.

Participants should employ good listening skills, such as those described in Anderson, Redman, and Rogers (1991) and Redman (1992), including paraphrasing, empathizing, asking open questions, asking clarifying questions, and nonverbal attending. Destructive criticism, ridicule, interrupting, and other rejecting behaviors should be avoided.

Finally, it is recommended that prior to the close of the discussion, participants share insights on *changes* in particular ideas and in the *patterns* of the responses as the discussion progresses. For example, participants may initially take the view of the student but through discussion may come to support the teacher's perspective (or vice versa) in a given case. Your instructor may ask you to record these changes in writing.

Conclusion

Be assured that the cases you are about to examine represent real problems related to the most critical components of teaching in today's elementary, middle, and high schools—components grounded in sound research and an extensive knowledge base. The purpose of this Casebook is to focus on diversity, equity, and social justice issues in teaching and learning, thereby raising awareness, elevating dialogue, and promoting action planning, all of which will increase your cultural competence and hence, your overall effectiveness in the classroom. Be creative as you explore issues in the cases, relate the issues to field experiences or teaching experiences, design cases of your own, and utilize insights thus derived as you develop lesson and unit plans. This process helps good teachers learn and grow and become even better—it is the epitome of professional development.

Readings for Extending Thinking

Aaronsohn, E., Howell, M., & Carter, C. J. (1995). Preparing monocultural teachers for a multicultural world: Attitudes toward inner-city schools. *Equity & Excellence in Education, 28*(1). Upper Saddle River, NJ: Prentice Hall.

Anderson, E. M., Redman, G. L., & Rogers, C. (1991). *Self-esteem for tots to teens.* Wayzata, MN: Parenting and Teaching Publications. Available at Parenting and Teaching for Self-Esteem, 1480 Arden View Drive, Arden Hills, MN 55112.

Banks, J. A., & Banks, C. A. M. (2001). *Multicultural education: Issues and perspectives.* New York: Wiley.

Clark, C., & Lampert, M. (1986). The study of teacher thinking: Implications for teacher education. *Journal of Teacher Education, 37*, 27–31.

Cooper, J. M. (1995). *Teacher's problem solving: A casebook of award-winning cases.* Boston: Allyn & Bacon.

Darling-Hammond, L. (2000, May/June). How teacher education matters. *Journal of Teacher Education.* Vol. 51, No. 3, 166–173

Darling-Hammond, L., & Snyder, J. (1998). Authentic assessment of teaching in context. In *Contextual teaching and learning: Preparing teachers to enhance student success in the workplace and beyond.* Office of Educational Research and Improvement. Washington, DC.

Gordon, E. W. (1990). Coping with communicentric bias. *Educational Researcher, 19.*

Grant, C. A. (1994). Challenging the myths about multicultural education. *Multicultural Education, 2*(2), 4–9.

Hunt, D. E., & Sullivan, E. V. (1974). *Between psychology and education.* New York: Holt, Rinehart and Winston.

Kennedy, M. M. (1991) *An agenda for research on teacher learning.* (Special Report). East Lansing, MI: National Center for Research on Teacher Learning.

Kleinfeld, J. (1992). Learning to think like a teacher: The study of cases. In J. H. Schulman (Ed.), *Case methods in teacher education* (pp. 33–49). New York: Teachers College Press.

McLaren, P. (1989). *Life in schools: An introduction to critical pedagogy in the foundations of education.* White Plains, NY: Longman.

McNergney, R., Herbert, J., & Ford, R. (1993). *Anatomy of a team case competition.* Paper presented at the annual meeting of the American Educational Research Association, Atlanta, Georgia.

McNergney, R., Herbert, J., & Ford, R. (1994). Cooperation and competition in case-based education. *Journal of Teacher Education, 45*(5).

Merseth, K. K. (1991). *The case for cases in teacher education*. Washington, DC: American Association for Higher Education and the American Association of Colleges for Teacher Education.

Morine-Dershimer, G. (1991). Learning to think like a teacher. *Teaching and Teacher Education, 7*(2), 159–168.

Oja, S., & Sprinthall, N. A. (1978). Psychological and moral development for teachers. In N. A. Sprinthall & R. L. Mosher (Eds.), *Value development as the aim of education* (pp. 117–134). Schenectady, NY: Charter Press.

Peterson, P. L., Carpenter, T., & Fennema, E. (1989). Teacher's knowledge of student's knowledge in mathematics problem solving: Correlational and case analysis. *Journal of Educational Psychology, 81*, 558–569.

Pusch, M. D. (Ed.). (1979). *Multicultural education: A cross-cultural training approach*. Yarmouth, ME: Intercultural press.

Redman, G. L. (1992). *Building self-esteem in students: A skill and strategy workbook for teachers*. Wayzata, MN: Parenting and Teaching for Self-Esteem. Available at parenting and Teaching for Self-Esteem, 1480 Arden View Drive, Arden Hills, MN 55112.

Schon, D. A. (1987). *Educating the reflective practitioner*. San Francisco: Jossey-Bass.

Shulman, L. (1992). Toward a pedagogy of cases. In J. H. Shulman (Ed.), *Case methods in teacher education* (p. x). New York: Teachers College Press.

Sprinthall, N. A., & Theis-Sprinthall, L. (1983). *The teacher as an adult learner: A cognitive-developmental view*. National Society for the Study of Education Yearbook (Pt. 2), 13–35.

Weiner, L. (1999). *Urban teaching: The essentials*. New York: Teachers College Press.

Internet Sites for Extending Thinking

http://www.adl.org
Anti-Defamation League materials on fighting prejudice and racism.

http://ublib.buffalo.edu/libraries/projects/cases/case.html
University at Buffalo, collection of several hundred cases and teaching notes in the
    natural sciences.

http://www.qual.auckland.ac.nz/case yin, %20 R.K.
Contains a list of references on case study research in various disciplines.

http://www.edchange.org/multicultural
The multicultural pavilion offers lists, tools, fact sheets poems, songs, research reports,
    and dialogue opportunities for educators and activists dedicated to equity, diversity,
    social justice and multicultural education.

http://hallway.org
A repository of teaching cases and other curriculum materials for faculty who teach
    public policy and related subjects, including education, environment, human services,
    urban issues, and international affairs. (From the Evans School of Public Affairs,
    University of Washington.)

http://mings.info-science.uiowa.edu/~stevens/cripted/page1.htm
Provides an overview of critical pedagogy and brief description of prominent theorists
    including Freire and Giroux.

Chapter 2

Gender

Introduction

Many, perhaps most, teachers are aware of the various forms of gender bias, the ways in which it is perpetuated, and its impact on both boys and girls in schools. For some, however, gender equity is still elusive. Many scholars believe that gender bias lowers student self-confidence, contributes to academic failure, and even leads to emotional and physical violence in the nation's schools.

Some educators are actively addressing such issues as sexism in the media, exclusion of women in curriculum, sexual harassment, date rape, teaching practices that favor one gender over the other, promotional inequities, and use of gender-neutral terms (e.g., "students" rather than "you guys"). Others are less knowledgeable and less concerned. In a recent conversation with several experienced and well-respected veteran teachers, awareness of issues related to racism seemed broadbased. When asked about sexism, however, knowledge seemed limited i.e., they related only to the issue of sexual harassment. They seemed unaware of other important gender-related issues such as those just mentioned.

It is critical that teacher educators explore thoughts and feelings about gender biases, raise awareness and understanding of the key issues, and help prospective and current teachers think about strategies for countering such biases, both on personal and institutional (e.g., school and community) levels. The cases in Chapter 2, "Gender," provide an opportunity to explore and think more broadly and deeply about gender-based issues as they relate to curriculum, instruction, and student behavior management in the classrooms and schools. Discussions of the cases in this section often invoke key terms and phrases such as:

critical thinking	sexism
discrimination	social-emotional classroom climate
gender equity	teacher flexibility and responsiveness
prejudice	teacher–student interaction patterns
reinforcement (of learning and/or behavior)	traditional social and role concepts
relevant curriculum	wait time

Definitions of key terms are located in the glossary of this text.

Case 1

Reinforcing Specifically

Students perform assigned tasks in a class activity and receive encouragement and praise from their teacher for their efforts.

It was the last week of school before the spring break. For the past two weeks, Ms. Bell's class had worked hard on a series of lab experiments focused on factors affecting the growth rate of seeds and young pea plants. The students had demonstrated pride in learning about the structure and function of seeds and in getting their seeds to grow.

On this particular Monday, as students were completing the final lab in the series, Ms. Bell circulated throughout the room, acknowledging individual contributions to the groups of four. "I want to tell you how proud I am of your work," she said to the members of one group. "Randolf and Jon, you did especially well in creating hypotheses prior to testing the effects of temperature and light. Your ideas took into account our prior learning and at the same time were creative. Mia and Amy, your work in recording the data for your group is commendable. Your records are easier to read because they are so neatly done."

As Ms. Bell walked away, Jon leaned over to Mia and Amy and quietly said, "I told you that boys were smarter. If we had listened to you two, Ms. Bell would have said our group was stupid." He concluded this statement by giving Randolf a high five. Mia shot back with, "Well at least Ms. Bell can read what we wrote down. You write like a preschooler!"

To the second group, Ms. Bell said, "Rod and Chang, your predictions as to what would happen in all of the labs in this unit were right on target! You have a good grasp of the principles of plant growth. And Sonya and Angie, your help in organizing the materials for the experiments and in checking the measurements of the plants was great. Your group couldn't have gotten the correct results without you!"

Ms. Bell moved to the third group. "Peter and José, your data analysis skills were excellent! Mary and Belle, you made some great drawings of the physical changes." The two girls looked at each other and smiled.

Ms. Bell provided similar feedback to the remaining two groups. All of the students seemed appreciative of her comments.

About five minutes before the bell was to ring, Ms. Bell reminded the students of their responsibilities for cleanup and the storage of lab materials. "Be sure you water your plants and return them to the window," she said. The students seemed to know their responsibilities, and they moved to store their plants and clear their tables.

Questions for Reflection

1. What was effective about Ms. Bell's interaction with students in this case?
2. Assume that the reinforcement pattern evident in these exchanges is typical of the feedback given by Ms. Bell during the term. What effect would you suspect Ms. Bell's interaction would have on the following?
   a. Her students' achievements
   b. Their feelings of pride in their work
   c. Their self-expectations for learning in science
   d. The culture for learning in the classroom
3. What, if anything, should the teacher do to change the dynamics of the science activities?

Activities for Extending Thinking

1. Teach a lesson in an accessible school—if you are currently in a field experience or are teaching, you may want to teach your lesson in that school. Videotape the lesson and analyze the tape for patterns of teacher–student interaction. Are there individuals and/or groups of students with whom you have more or less interaction? What types of interactions do you have with various individuals and groups (e.g., interactions that stimulate higher levels of thinking)? List the interaction patterns you have identified. Be prepared to share in class.
2. Examine local, state, and/or national standards for teacher education and identify the standards that relate to the key issues in this case.

Case 2

Fridays Are Video Days

A teacher attends to student socializing during the Friday video.

It was Friday and Ms. Hanson loaded another videotape on the Apollo space project into the videocassette recorder. It was her opinion that if the students worked hard all week, they should be rewarded with a video each Friday. In addition to serving as a reward, the videos also varied the stimulus.

Students who were not interested in the Friday video had the option of working on an extra-credit project related to the current unit of study. This month the unit was on mass and volume. On this particular Friday, Jenny, Desweon, and Ann had opted to do extra credit rather than watch the tape. In fact, the same group had chosen to do extra credit for the past three weeks.

This Friday was no different from other recent Fridays in that a group of four or five boys in the back of the room had again begun to talk during the video. For some reason, they had come to equate video watching with socializing.

To curb their talking, Ms. Hanson used proximity. Taking a seat next to the group allowed her to give them her full attention. From her vantage point, she could also see the students working on extra credit. If a student in that group raised his or her hand for help, she could motion to the student to come to her.

When Jenny and Ann raised their hands, Ms. Hanson waved for them to come to her. Jenny pointed to a problem at the end of the chapter. "I don't get number 8," she said. "Me either," added Ann. "Let's take a look," replied Ms. Hanson. "What part *do* you understand?"

As Jenny began to respond, Ms. Hanson interrupted. "Hold that thought." She leaned toward Todd and Tim and, with her finger to her lips, said, "Shhh, please, I've asked you before not to talk during the videos. Every time I have to ask you, it takes away from the time I could be helping someone." She waited until the boys quieted down.

When she turned to Jenny, she apologized. "Sorry. Where were we?" Jenny reminded her and they began again.

Ten minutes later, Teresa raised her hand. Ms. Hanson motioned for her to come over. Teresa complained that Todd was talking so loud that she couldn't hear the video. Ms. Hanson reminded the boys to be quiet again.

That evening, on the way home from school, Ms. Hanson wondered about the Friday arrangement. She thought of the patterns of behavior so typical of Fridays, including having to spend much of the period with the boys in the back of the room. She listed the pros: giving the student choices (to view the video or do extra credit), varying the weekly activity routine, rewarding student work, and giving personal attention to those who need it. Maybe the Friday arrangement was fine after all.

Questions for Reflection

1. Respond to Ms. Hanson's rationale for maintaining Fridays as days that students can choose to either watch an educational video or complete extra credit work. Do you agree or disagree with her practice? Why?
2. If you would change her Friday video activity, how would you do so? Give a rationale for any changes you suggest.
3. What moral/ethical issues, if any, are raised in this case?

Activities for Extending Thinking

1. Design a student survey that elicits pupil opinion about the use of a particular classroom activity such as the "video day" activity. What questions would you ask?
2. List two or three ideas around which you could develop cases (stories with problems) that you could use in classes you might teach. Begin by listing the key information e.g., about history or biology, or literature, you want students to obtain or develop, then briefly outline a story that creates in students the desire to obtain or construct that information.
3. Examine local, state, and/or national standards for teacher education and identify the standard or standards that relate to the key issues in this case.

Case 3

Developing Skills of Critical Analysis: Exposing the Myths of Films and Fairy Tales*

A teacher guides students in the exposing of myths that perpetuate common societal stereotypes and in using writing and speaking as vehicles for change.

Ms. Christensen wanted her students to develop the tools necessary to critique major ideas in terms of the degree to which they contribute to, or distract from, the building of a just society. To this end, each year her class embarked on a journey of analyzing cartoons, children's movies, and stories.

This year she planned to begin by reading to the class Ariel Dorfman's *The Emperor's Old Clothes: What the Lone Ranger, Babar, and Other Innocent Heroes Do to Our Minds*, in which the author claims that both popular literature and children's literature perpetuate existing power structures and deny the possibility of greater equality.

Next, as the first step in dismantling old values and constructing more just ones, the class would critique cartoons and children's movies, including *Bugs Bunny, Daffy Duck, 101 Dalmatians, Pocahontas, The Lion King, Dinosaurs, The Emperor's New Groove, Sleeping Beauty, Cinderella*, and *Snow White*. The class would identify roles of people of color, as well as of men and women in the films. They would look at the power relationships among the characters; listen for loaded words, such as "backward," "primitive," and "lazy"; and consider the effect of the story on the self-image of members of a diverse audience.

In the final leg of the journey, students would share their critiques with audiences beyond the classroom. Such a step would suggest to students that their efforts were of larger import and indeed might lead to changes in their school, community, or state. Some students wrote a pamphlet to distribute to parents serving on school advisory boards, while others watched Saturday-morning cartoons and wrote a report card for each. (Popeye received an F because of its portrayal of ethnic groups as stupid and Americans as superior, and Teenage Mutant Ninja Turtles received a D because of its focus on using violence to solve problems.)

Ms. Christensen noted that each year most students looked deeper into the issues and understood, for example, the master–servant relationship or how the images affected the dreams and goals of viewers or readers. A few, however, shrugged their shoulders and suggested that being rich or poor is okay, or that kids just read or view fairy tales as fun and do not really internalize the values portrayed. Ms. Christensen recalled occasional statements from students such as "Just because girls see Tinker Bell or Cinderella with tiny waists doesn't mean they'll want one." She wondered, "How can I determine how many of my students hold on to societal stereotypes and how firmly they hold them? How can I assess the degree to which my students are developing the knowledge, skills, and dispositions for thinking critically?"

Questions for Reflection

1. What did you find effective about Ms. Christensen's use of literature and movies to teach values?
2. How would you address society's perceptions of beauty, age, and personal goals with your students?
3. How can Ms. Christensen determine the degree to which her class believes that stereotypes in media are not harmful?
4. How can Ms. Christensen determine if students are improving in their ability to think critically as they participate in this unit of instruction? (Draw on your knowledge about performance assessment, authentic assessment, and portfolios in responding to this question.)
5. Is it appropriate for teachers to challenge students' traditional social and role concepts, e.g., learn alternatives gender roles, especially those based on family and religious values? If so, at what ages and by what methods?

Activities for Extending Thinking

1. Discuss with a parent, a teacher, and an administrator his/her philosophy about teaching values, particularly values embedded in traditional fairy tales and children's literature. Discuss both the process (methods) of teaching values and the content of the values themselves. Include the previous "Questions for Reflection" in your discussions.
2. Critique television programs and/or commercials for their underlying values. What specific messages are sent to the viewer about gender roles?
3. Discuss with students the impact of fairy tales on conceptualizations about gender in their lives and the lives of people they know. Record your insights, and be prepared to summarize your findings in class.
4. Outline a unit plan or a series of lesson plans that would promote healthy values in a class that you might teach. Relate your product to local, state, and/or national standards for teacher education.

*Credit for the idea on which this case is based is given to: Christensen, L. (1994). Unlearning the myths that bind us. In *Rethinking our classrooms*, special edition of *Rethinking Schools* (pp. 8–13). Milwaukee, WI: Rethinking Schools Limited.

Dwight, What Do You Think?

After reading a story to his class, a teacher uses a variety of questioning strategies to engage students in discussion.

Mr. Beach was beginning the third week of his first year of full-time teaching at the middle school. He had enjoyed the two years that he had been a substitute teacher, and he was excited about having his own class for the first time. His fifth hour was his favorite—a class of 25 highly motivated students who were limited in English proficiency.

Mr. Beach believed strongly in the need to develop a sense of community in his class. During the first week of September, he had the class learn and practice group membership skills, including good listening skills. The students had demonstrated a high level of proficiency in using the new skills, and they seemed to have begun to feel a sense of unity as a class. In both large and small groups, students were cooperative with Mr. Beach and with one another. Now, in the third week of school, the class was reading *Love You Forever* by Robert Munsch. Mr. Beach's primary goals were to (1) help students improve in reading comprehension and (2) learn to enjoy reading. He began by having students recall previously acquired knowledge.

"Class," he said, "tell me, does it seem to you that the son used good listening skills?"

Several students raised their hands. Mr. Beach called on Dwight, an African-American student who sat in the front row.

"No," Dwight replied.

"What makes you say 'no'?" asked Mr. Beach.

Dwight appeared to be thinking.

After a few seconds, Mr. Beach asked, "What are the good listening skills that we learned? Let's review."

Dwight replied, "Looking at the person, but not staring, not interrupting, and being able to repeat what the person said."

"Excellent!" said Mr. Beach. "Now, as far as we can determine, did the little boy who grew up to be a man use these kinds of skills?"

"Yes," replied Dwight. "'Cause he was able to say 'I'll love you forever' to his mother when she got old, so he must have listened to it when he was growing up."

"Exactly," said Mr. Beach. "Now, class, why couldn't his mother finish the saying when she was old? Mary?"

Mary thought a couple of seconds and then answered, "I'm not sure."

"Dara, what do you think?" asked Mr. Beach.

"Cause she was too old," answered Dara.

"Mahmoud, what do you think about Dara's answer?"

Mahmoud responded, "Well, she was sick, too."

"Yes, and when people get sick they get weak, don't they, sometimes too weak to talk, right?" asked Mr. Beach. Looking at Mahmoud, Mr. Beach continued, "Have you known anyone who was old and sick and almost too weak to talk?"

Mahmoud proceeded to tell the class about his grandfather who had been ill for several weeks with the flu.

Several other students mentioned persons they had known who had been ill. They talked of being sad when a loved one was ill. The discussion continued to engage the students. They completely lost track of time. Mr. Beach was pleased about the students' understanding of the story, as well as their ability to connect to prior learning. Moreover, he was pleased with his ability to lead a good, lively, and productive discussion.

Questions for Reflection

1. Assess the teacher's proficiency at using discussion and questioning techniques. What, if anything, did he do well? What positive effects did each action have on students?
2. Specifically, how (if at all) should he change his approach?
3. What would a teacher want to know prior to using materials related to death and dying?

Activity for Extending Thinking

1. Review at least one resource in the Readings for Extending Thinking at the end of Chapter 2. Summarize your insights in writing.

Case 5

Integrating Women's Issues into Curriculum

*A student challenges a teacher's assignment that requires them
to research important women in history.*

Ms. Williams had just completed teaching her class about how to conduct research using library and Internet resources. So that her students could apply the research skills that they had learned, she devised an assignment about important women in history. Her goals were twofold: first, to learn about the often-overlooked accomplishments of women, and second, to allow students to see firsthand the value of knowing how to apply research skills.

Ms. Williams brought the assignment sheet and the rubric to be used in grading it. As she was handing out the assignment sheet and explaining the requirements for the project, she was interrupted by a comment from the back of the room. "No way," said Sam. "I'm not doing a report on a stupid girl!"

"Hey, girls aren't stupid!" Savannah replied.

Other students mumbled as Ms. Williams tried to regain control of her classroom. "That's enough," she said. The room quieted down.

Ms. Williams explained that each student, with no exceptions, needed to pick a woman about whom to do a project. Sam sunk down in his chair with a frown. Ms. Williams finished handing out the papers and excused the students for lunch.

Questions for Reflection

1. What could Ms. Williams have done ahead of time to prevent potential opposition to the assignment?
2. Was her response to Sam's comment adequate? What else, if anything, should she have said or done?
3. What message(s) do you think the students got from the above interaction that day? How do you think they felt upon leaving class?
4. Within your subject matter area, list important contributions of women that you would want your students to know about.

Activities for Extending Thinking

1. Outline a lesson plan in your subject matter major that involves the contributions of a woman or women to your subject matter area. Incorporate in the lesson how you will prevent potential opposition and set the stage for a positive learning experience. Identify the local, state, and national standards your lesson will address.
2. Select a course that you might teach, e.g., biology grade 10, English grade 7, or a portion of an elementary program, e.g., science grade 3. In that subject matter area, list important women that you would want students to know about and the accomplishments of each.

Design Your Own Case

Gender

Drawing on your personal experiences as a P–12 pupil, or those from a clinical experience in a school, design a case that explores an issue of gender in the classroom. The story can focus on a method or strategy related to a single subject matter area (e.g., English or social studies) or on a more generic method or strategy pertinent to a wider range of subject matter areas. Your issue might also relate to:

- Planning and preparation
- Classroom environment
- Instruction
- Teacher responsibilities*

Include some demographic data that tell a bit about the community, school, classroom, teacher, students, and curriculum. Include at least one problem for which there is no obvious answer. Use fictitious names of persons and schools to maintain confidentiality. Your case should be approximately two pages in length (typed, double-spaced) and should include three to four Questions for Reflection, and one or two Activities for Extending Thinking. Go to Resource C and use the form to design your own case.

*The four categories are from Danielson, C. (1996). *Enhancing professional practice: A framework for teaching*. Alexandria, VA: Association for Supervision and Curriculum Development.

Readings for Extending Thinking

Alarcon, N., Castro, R., Perez, E., Pesquera, B., Riddell, A.S., & Zavella, P. (Eds.). (1993). *Chicana critical issues*. Berkeley, CA: Third Woman Press.

American Association of University Women. (1996). *Girls in the middle. Working to succeed in school*. Washington, DC: American Association of University Women.

Andersen, M. L., & Collins, P. H. (Eds.). (1995). *Race, class, and gender: An anthology* (2nd ed.). Belmont, CA: Wadsworth.

Arias, A., Jr., & Bellman, B. (1990). Computer-mediated classrooms for culturally and linguistically diverse learners. *Computers in the schools, 7*(1–2), 227–241.

Baca Zinn, M., & Dill, B. T. (Eds.). (1994). *Woman of color in U.S. society*. Philadelphia: Temple University Press.

Bailey, D. F., & Paisley, P. O. (2004). Developing and nurturing excellence in African-American male adolescents. *Journal of counseling and Development, 82*, 10–17.

Barbieri, M. (1995). *Sounds from the heart: Listening to girls*. New Hampshire: Heinemann.

Barnett, R. C., & Rivers, C. (2004). *Some differences: How gender myths are hurting our relationships, our children, and our jobs*. New York: Basic Books.

Belenky, M. F., Clinchy, B. M., Goldberg, N. R., & Tarrule, F. M. (1986). *Woman's ways of knowing: The development of self, voice, and mind*. New York: Basic Books.

Bilken, S. K., & Pollard, D. (1993). *Gender and education*. Chicago: University of Chicago Press.

Blais, M. (1995). *In these girls hope is a muscle*. New York: Atlantic Monthly Press.

Bly, R. (1990). *Iron John: A book about men*. Reading, MA: Addison-Wesley.

Boyd, H., & Allen, R. L. (Eds.). (1995). *Brotherman: The odyssey of Black men in America—An anthology*. New York: Ballantine.

Brown, L. (1998). *Raising their voices: The politics of girls' anger*. Cambridge, MA: Harvard University Press.

Burbridge, L. (1991). *The interaction of race, gender and socioeconomic status in education outcomes*. Wellesley, MA: Center for Research on Women.

Campbell, P. B., & Sanders, J. (2002). Challenging the system: Assumptions and data behind the push for single-sex schools. In A. Datnow & L. Hubbard (Eds.), *Gender in policy and practice: Perspectives on single-sex and coeducational schooling* (pp. 31–46). New York: Routledge Falmer.

Castillo-Speed, L. (Ed.). (1995). *Latina: Women's voices from the borderlands*. New York: Touchstone/Simon & Schuster.

Chapman, A. (1997). *A great balancing act: Equitable education for girls and boys.* Washington, DC: National Association of Independent Schools.

Crawford, S. H. (1996). *Beyond dolls and guns: 101 ways to help children avoid gender bias.* New Hampshire: Heinemann.

Cunningham, M. (1999). African-American adolescent males' perceptions of their community resources and constraints: A longitudinal analysis. *Journal of Community Psychology, 27*(5), 569–588.

de la Torre, A., & Pesquera, B. M. (1993). *Building with our hands: New directions in Chicana studies.* Berkeley, CA: University of California Press.

Douglas, S. J. (1994). *Where the girls are: Growing up female with the mass media.* New York: Times Books.

DuBois, E., & Ruiz, V. (Eds.). (1994). *Unequal sisters: A multicultural reader in U.S. women's history* (2nd ed.). New York: Routledge.

Dyer, G., & Tiggemann, M. (1996). The effect of school environment on body concerns in adolescent woman. *Sex Roles, 34*(12), 127–138.

Eder, D., Evans, C., & Parker, S. (1995). *Schooltalk: Gender and adolescent culture.* New Brunswick, NJ: Rutgers University Press.

Ferguson, A. A. (2001). *Bad boys: Public schools in the making of Black masculinity.* Ann Arbor, MI: University of Michigan Press.

Fordham, S. (1996). *Blacked out: Dilemmas of race, identity, and success at Capital High.* Chicago: University of Chicago Press.

Fordham, S. (1997). *A low score wins: Is high self-esteem compromising Black girls' academic achievement?* Paper presented at the RISE Conference Proceedings. New Brunswick, NJ: Rutgers University, October 1999.

Frankenberg, R. (1993). *White women, race matters: The social construction of whiteness.* Minneapolis, MN: University of Minnesota Press.

Froschl, M., Sprung, B., & Mullin-Ridler, N. (1998). *Quit it!: A teacher's guide on teasing and bullying for use with students in grades K-3.* New York: Equity Concepts; Wellesley, MA: Wellesley College Center for Research on Women; Washington, DC: NEA.

Garbarino, J. (1999). *Lost boys: Why our sons turn violent and how we can save them.* New York: Free Press.

Gaskell, J., & Willinsky, J. (1995). *Gender informs curriculum.* NY: Teachers College Press.

Gilligan, J. (1997). *Violence: Reflections on a national epidemic.* New York: Vintage.

Guy-Sheftall, B. (Ed.). (1995). *Words of fire: An anthology of African-American feminist thought.* New York: New Press.

Harris, L., & Associates, Inc. (1993). *Hostile hallways: The AAUW survey on sexual harassment in America's schools.* Washington, DC: American Association of University Women.

Hine, D. C., King, W., & Reed, L. (Eds.). (1995). *We specialize in the wholly impossible: A reader in Black women's history.* Brooklyn, NY: Carlson.

Katz, J. (Ed.). (1995). *Messengers of the wind: Native American women tell their life stories.* New York: Ballantine.

Kivel, P. (1999). *Boys will be men: Raising our sons for courage, caring, and community.* British Columbia, Canada: New Society.

Kleinfeld, J. (1999). Student performance: Males versus females. *The Public Interest, 134* (Winter), 3–20.

Kramer, S. (1988). Sex role stereotyping: How it happens and how to avoid it. In A. O'Brien Carelli (Ed.), *Sex equity in education* (pp. 5–23). Springfield, IL: Charles C. Thomas.

Lee, V.E. (1997). Gender equity and the organization of schools. In B. J. Bank & P. M. Hall (Eds.), *Gender, equity, and schooling: Policy and practice.* New York: Garland.

Li Nim-Yu, K. (1990). *Writing with pen or computer? A study on ESL secondary school learners.* (ERIC Document Reproduction Service No. ED 322–720)

Maher, F.A., & Tetreault, M. K. (1994). *The feminist classroom.* New York: Basic.

Mid-Atlantic Equity Center. (1999). *Adolescent Boys: Statistics and Trends* (A fact sheet). Chevy Chase, MD: Mid-Atlantic Equity Assistance Center.

Mosca, G. N., & Shmurak, C. B. (1995). An interdisciplinary, gender equitable mathematics project for the middle school. *Middle School Journal, 27*(1), 26–29.

National Coalition for Women and Girls in Education. (2002, June). *Title IX at 30: Report card on gender equity.* Washington, DC: Author.

National Research Council. (1996). *National science education standards.* Washington, DC: National Academy Press.

Oakes, J. (1985). *Keeping track: How schools structure inequality.* New Haven, CT: Yale University Press.

Odean, K. (1997). *Great books for girls.* New York: Ballantine.

Orenstein, P. (1994). *Schoolgirls: Young women, self-esteem, and the confidence gap.* New York: Doubleday.

Perry, E. L., Schmidtke, J. M., & Kulik, C. T. (1998). Propensity to sexually harass: An exploration of gender differences. *Sex Roles: A Journal of Research 38*(5–6), 443–460.

Peterson, S. (2002). Gender meanings in eighth grade: Students talk about classroom writing. *Gender and Education, 14*(4), 351–366.

Pipher, M. (1994). *Reviving Ophelia: Saving the selves of adolescent girls.* New York: Ballantine.

Ravitch, D. (1996, November 18). Stereotype bashing. *Forbes, 203.*

Rosser, S. V. (1995). *Teaching the majority: Breaking the gender barrier in science, mathematics, and engineering.* New York: Teacher College Press.

Sadker, D. (1999). Gender equity: Still knocking at the classroom door. *Educational Leadership, 56*(7), 22–26.

Sadker, M., & Sadker, D. (1994). *Failing at fairness: How America's schools cheat girls.* New York: Scribner's.

Sadker, M. P., & Sadker, D. M. (2004). Gender bias: From colonial America to today's classrooms. In J. A. Banks & C. A. M. Banks (Eds.), *Multicultural education: Issues and perpectives* (5th ed., pp. 135–163). Hoboken, NJ: Wiley.

Salisbury, J., & Jackson, D. (1996). *Challenging macho values: Practical ways of working with adolescent boys.* London: Falmer.

Sanders, J., & Rocco, S. (1994). *Bibliography on gender equity in mathematics, science, and technology: Resources for classroom teachers.* New York: Center for Advanced Study in Education, CUNY Graduate Center.

Scantlebury, K., Johnson, E., Lykens, S., Bailey, B., Clements, R., Gleason, S., Lewis, R., & Letts, W. (1996, January). *Creating a cycle of equitable teaching.* Paper presented at the annual meeting of the Association for the Education of Teachers in Science, Seattle, WA.

Shmurak, C. B. (1994a). Girls' high schools—How empowering have they been? *The High School Journal, 78*(1), 1–12.

Shmurak, C. B. & Ratliff, T. M. (1994). Gender equity and gender bias: Issues for the middle school teacher. *Middle School Journal, 25*(5), 63–66.

Silverstein, O., & Rashbaum, B. (1994). *The courage to raise good men.* New York: Penguin.

Streitmatter, J. (1994). *Toward gender equity in the classroom.* Albany, NY: SUNY Press.

Titus, J. J. (1993). Gender messages in education foundations textbooks. *Journal of Teacher Education, 44*(1), 38–43.

Tovey, R. (1995, July/August). A narrowly gender-based model of learning may end up cheating all students. *Harvard Education Letter,* 3–6.

Tyson, C. A., & Hinton-Johnson, K. (January/February, 2003). Once upon a time: Teaching about women and social justice through literature. *Social Education, 67*(1), 54–57.

Wellesley Center for Research on Women. (1992). *How schools shortchange girls: A study of major findings on girls and education.* Washington, DC: American Association of University Women.

Internet Sites for Extending Thinking

http://www.aauw.org
American Association of University Women materials on promoting gender equality.

http://www.aauw.org/research/GGES.pdf
Gender Gaps Executive Summary for PDF.

http://www.aauw.org/ef/harass/pdf/completeguide.pdf
Harassment-Free Hallways.

http://www.aauw.org/research/girls_education/hostile93cfm
The AAUW Survey on Sexual Harassment in America's schools (1993).

http://www.nmwh.org
History of women's suffrage.

http://www.greatwomen.org
Women who have contributed to American society; teaching ideas.

http://www.nwhp.org
Clearinghouse for women's history; resources, programs, and events.

http://www.looksmart.com
Type "men's issues" in the "Search the Web" box and click on "Search"—links to library resources, including health and sexuality, publication for men.

www.centerforlearning.org
    The Center for Learning
    21590 Center Ridge Road
    Rocky River, Ohio 44116

www.activecitizenship.org
    Center for Multicultural Cooperation
    P.O. Box 1385
    Coarsegold, California 93614

www.charactercounts.orvccwelcome.htm
    Character Counts!
    Josephson Institute of Ethics
    4640 Admiralty Way, Suite 1001
    Marina del Rey, California 90292-6610

www.ethicsusa.com
    Character Education Center
    P.O. Box 80208
    Rancho Santa Margarita, California 92688-0208

Chapter 3

Ethnicity

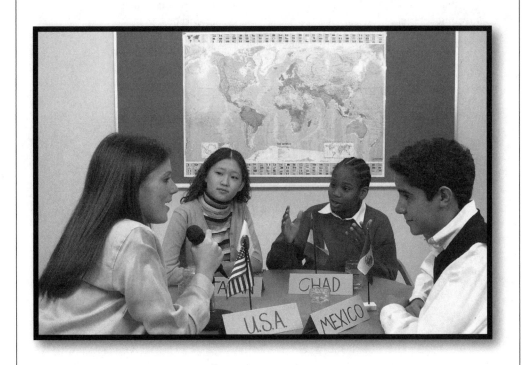

Introduction

Ethnicity is used in this text to refer to a group of people, of common national origin or origins (Gollnick & Chinn, 2004). Ethnicity is viewed here as a subgroup of race, e.g., the ethnic groups of Cambodian, Chinese, Japanese, Thai, and Vietnamese are considered subgroups of the Asian racial category (Adams, et al., 1997). Though White students often think of themselves as White or "American," their ethnic heritage (country of origin) may actually be French, German, Irish, Italian, Swedish, and the like. Similarly, a Black student may be ethnically French, German, or of any other country of origin.

Chapter 3 contains cases that help us think about similarities and differences in students related to their ethnic heritage. Typically, discussions of important ethnic considerations such as those in this section include key terms and concepts such as:

cultural competence	interdisciplinary teaching
cultural norms	learning styles
culture	multiculturalism
democracy in the classroom	rule consequences
ethnic group	social justice curriculum
ethnocentrism	stereotype

Definitions of key terms are located in the glossary of this text.

Case 6

Let's All Make Up the Rules for Our Classroom

Students are given the opportunity to make real decisions regarding the operation of their classroom by helping to formulate rules for behavior.

It was the first day of the new school year. After greeting his students and describing his course goals, Mr. Chu split the class into small groups. He explained to the students that since this was their classroom as well as his, they could help make the rules for conduct. He told each group to write out several rules to recommend to the class, as well as a consequence for breaking each rule. He monitored all the groups, making notes on each student's participation. After the groups completed the assignment, he collected their lists.

That evening he reviewed the lists and developed five rules that captured some aspects of each list. He stated the rules positively; for example, if a group had written "Never talk while someone else is talking," Mr. Chu wrote "Respect others," and he gave written examples, such as "Listen when others are talking." He also included the consequence of breaking each rule, such as time-outs, loss of privileges, and detention.

When he had finished compiling the class list, he recalled that a number of the students had not participated in formulating rules and consequences for the class. He had not pressed them to contribute when he monitored the groups, but he was curious why they chose not to help create the rules. He noted further that two of the students were of Russian heritage, one a male, one a female. Another two were female students from Cambodia. Mr. Chu wondered whether cultural values, such as respect for and even dependence on adult authority, might have been the reason for their lack of participation. He would ask them when he had a chance.

The next day, Mr. Chu explained how he had arrived at five collective class rules and consequences. After the class agreed that the list was acceptable, Mr. Chu wrote the rules in large letters on a sign and posted it at the front of the classroom. He felt confident that by having ownership in the rules, students would be more likely to follow them.

Mr. Chu reminded the students that the next 10 minutes would be devoted to silent reading. He thought to himself, "Now would be the time to have a friendly chat with each of the four students who did not help make up the class rules." He knew he needed to be clear that he was not disappointed in them, but rather that he merely was interested in understanding why they did not participate.

Questions for Reflection

1. Was Mr. Chu rightfully concerned about the international students, or was he over-reacting?
2. If the students answered "I don't know" when asked why they did not participate, what would you recommend Mr. Chu say? Is it permissible for these students not to participate in activities like this one?
3. Develop a student behavior management plan that you could implement in your classroom, including the following:
    a. How you would involve all students in developing the rules and procedures for classroom behavior
    b. The rules and procedures that you would hope to develop (with or without student involvement), i.e., any nonnegotiable rules
    c. The positive consequences of honoring the rules or procedures
    d. The negative consequences of not honoring the rules or procedures
4. How would you feel if students did not follow their own rules? What would you say to students?

Activity for Extending Thinking

1. Interview a school administrator, a school counselor, and a teacher to determine their views on involving students of various ethnicities (some of whom may feel it is not their role to participate) in establishing expectations for classroom behavior. Summarize your findings in writing, and be prepared to share in class.

Case 7

Other Cultures Celebrate Thanksgiving, Too

Thanksgiving celebrations of five different cultures are compared in a small-group reading activity.

It was mid-November when Mr. Rodriguez began his lesson on "Giving Thanks in Different Lands." He read the lesson objectives from the blackboard to his class: "Today we will learn how people of the United States have celebrated 'Thanksgiving,' as well as how people of other countries give thanks."

"How many of you have ever celebrated Thanksgiving?" he asked. Nearly all of the students raised a hand. "Please take out a sheet of paper and write what you know about Thanksgiving celebrations. Your papers will not be graded. I just want to know what you already know about our topic."

After several minutes, it appeared that all had finished writing. Mr. Rodriguez collected the papers and then read a brief story, entitled "The First Thanksgiving," a traditional account of how English settlers in North America gave thanks for their good fortune. Mr. Rodriguez raised a number of questions about the historical accuracy of the account, including whether Native Americans typically would have helped in the celebration.

"Class, now that you have heard the usual story about the 'First Thanksgiving,' I would like to extend our thinking about celebrations of thanks. It turns out that Native Americans actually had such celebrations before the English arrived in this land." For the next few minutes, Mr. Rodriguez read a short story about the first fruits ceremony and the green corn ceremony of the Wampanoags of Plymouth, Massachusetts, noting the cultural significance of each celebration.

Now," he said, "I have stories of how four other cultures gave thanks for what they considered to be important. I have assigned pairs. I will give each pair two stories of Thanksgiving celebrations of people of other lands. I would like each of you to read one story to your partner. Take your time in reading. Your goal is to understand both of the stories completely. We will discuss them when everyone is done."

Mr. Rodriguez passed out the stories. They were "First Fruits," a celebration of the African Zulu; "Mid-Autumn Festival," the holiday of many Chinese people in San Francisco's Chinatown; "Día de Gracias," celebrated by native people of Mexico (including the Olmecas, Zapotecas, Mayas, Toltecas, Mixtecas, and Haustecas); and "Sukkot," or "Feast of the Tabernacles," celebrated by Jewish people.

When the students were finished reading to one another, Mr. Rodriguez asked them to share the key aspects of each celebration with the class. He recorded critical elements of each story in four columns on the board.

He then asked, "What are some similarities about how all four groups give thanks?" After listing several, he asked, "What are some differences?" Finally, as the period was drawing to a close, he asked, "What general principles have we learned about different groups of people and how they give thanks for what they have?" Again, he listed student responses on the board.

"And what have we learned about broadening our perspectives or extending our understanding of the meaning of 'First' in 'First Thanksgiving'?" Several pupils shared this views.

"Tomorrow," he concluded, "We will talk more about how you give thanks, as well as what today's lesson might mean to you personally. Good job today! See you tomorrow."

Questions for Reflection

1. What did Mr. Rodriguez do to extend students' knowledge about Thanksgiving celebrations? List the steps that he had students follow.
2. How would Mr. Rodriguez's method for presenting information help students learn how to think?
3. Describe other kinds of lessons that can contribute to goals of multiculturalism. Give an example of each kind of lesson.
4. If you wanted to teach your students about the injustices against Native Americans would you include it as part of this lesson or as a separate topic for another time?

Activities for Extending Thinking

1. Conduct a simple survey of persons of various ethnicities on the pros and cons of multiculturalism. Be prepared to summarize your findings for the class.
2. Discuss with practicing teachers methods they use for engaging students with content, or as some would say, methods for getting students to "actively construct meaning." For example, in teaching a skill, a teacher might tell about the skill, model (demonstrate) it, have students practice the skill with guidance, and then have students practice the skill independently. In teaching a concept, the teacher might define the concept, give examples and nonexamples of it, have students give examples and nonexamples, and have students demonstrate how to apply the concept. Ask the teachers how, if at all, they modify their teaching strategies to accommodate the needs of students of diverse backgrounds.

When Will I Ever Use This? Mathematics and Social Justice

A teacher designs an interdisciplinary math lesson that not only teaches graphing but also helps raise student awareness of social issues.

Ms. McMullen had taught fifth grade for five years. She was considered a competent teacher by her colleagues and students. One of her favorite subjects was math. She had kept up with developments in the field, including the use of manipulatives to help students engage in concrete activities. Moreover, she could really see that students were learning the content of the subject, and she knew it would be important in their lives as students in school and beyond.

Recently, Ms. McMullen had noticed a news report of a poll on perceptions of Whites and Blacks about the economic conditions of Blacks in the United States of America. As she began planning for her next unit on constructing and interpreting charts and graphs, she decided that by using the current data from the article, she could teach not only math (graphing), but also a lesson on race relations.

On the first day of her unit, Ms. McMullen introduced the academic objectives of the math unit, defined some key terms, and outlined the benefits of understanding the charts and graphs. She showed how to represent data in a bar graph, a line graph, and a pie chart.

She then assigned students the task of reading and summarizing the material from a recent study on racial attitudes that was conducted by a leading national newspaper, a well-known foundation, and a nationally respected university. Finally, she informed students that they should present the data in the form of a graph. They could follow any of the charts or graphs she had introduced, but they had to be able to defend their choice. She was curious to hear the rationales they would give.

In their graphs, students were to represent survey respondents in terms of race and to depict what they considered to be key findings of the survey—for example, that 68 percent of Blacks surveyed said that racism is a big problem in our society today, whereas only 38 percent of Whites thought so; and 46 percent of Whites said that Blacks on average hold jobs of equal quality to those of Whites, whereas government data show that Blacks on average earn 60 percent less than Whites.

Ms. McMullen planned to focus first on the mathematical aspects of the lesson and then later to connect those ideas with the issues surrounding the racial-attitude aspects of the activity.

Questions for Reflection

1. Would you support Ms. McMullen's efforts to integrate the two lessons (graphing and race relations)? Why or why not?
2. Would the cultural makeup of the class—for example, all White students, or a majority of students of color—affect your answer to question 1?
3. How might you design a lesson in your subject matter area in which you connect some "traditional" subject matter, such as graphing, reading, writing, or computing, with issues of social justice? Describe the lesson briefly. For example, a biology or health teacher might build a lesson around the Tuskegee Syphilis Experiment in which, between 1932 and 1972, 339 Black men were purposely given ineffective treatments for syphilis in a government effort to discover how the disease affected Blacks as compared to Whites—an activity later called "profoundly morally wrong and . . . clearly racist" by President Clinton. The lesson(s) could focus on both scientific and social justice issues. (http://infoplease.com/ipa/A0762136.html)

Activity for Extending Thinking

1. Interview at least two practicing teachers to learn the strategies they use to integrate social justice issues with subject matter content. Be prepared to summarize your findings in class.

Case 9

Overlook the Stereotypes—It's Art

A parent criticizes a display of photos of murals from the 1930s for depicting stereotypical images of African-Americans and women.

It was parent conference night and Ms. Lotzer was saying good night to her last parent visitor when he said to her, "By the way, those large photos with the world maps on the bulletin board, did you know that they contain stereotypical images of Africans in loincloths and 'pickaninny hairstyles'? And one has 'Aunt-Jemima–like' women picking cotton. They are really insulting!"

Ms. Lotzer responded, "You know, I never thought of that. Those are photos of murals that were donated to the school by the city. They're from a collection commissioned during the Depression years to employ out-of-work artists. They were thought to have artistic value. I thought they would be better for the children than blank walls, and they do accurately portray perceptions that existed in the 1930s."

"Well, that's true, but I don't think they send the right message! In fact, in addition to the ethnic stereotypes portrayed, three of them don't depict any female images at all!"

The next day, Ms. Lotzer shared her experience with the school principal. Sympathetic to the parent's concern, the principal ordered the photos covered until it was decided whether they should be permanently removed.

The following day in class, Ms. Lotzer's students asked, "Why are the photos covered?" She told them of the events of the previous day, being careful to maintain the anonymity of the parent involved. She also mentioned that the photos would remain covered until the next faculty meeting. "At that time, I will present the parent's concerns and I hope we can agree on a reasonable policy, but for now the pictures will be covered," she said.

Some of her students seemed to support the decision of the principal, while others did not agree with his decision to cover the photos. The students asked Ms. Lotzer, "What do you plan to do?"

"I'm not sure what I'll say," she replied. "It would also be helpful, though, to know what you think—both as individuals and as a class. It would be helpful to know what more parents think," she said. "Perhaps we could devise several survey questions for parents and compile the responses. Then, I can represent not only my own views, but also those of you and your parents. Are you willing to do that?" she asked.

Hearing no objection, Ms. Lotzer asked, "Who can think of a first question that we could include in our survey?"

Questions for Reflection

1. Do you agree or disagree with the principal's decision to cover the photos?
2. What principles should teachers follow in
   a. selecting materials for display in their classrooms?
   b. involving students and parents in decisions regarding such issues?
   c. countering stereotypes portrayed in other forms of media, such as television, magazines, newspapers, and electronic media, e.g., the Internet?
3. Did Ms. Lotzer overstep her authority in surveying students and parents without authorization from the principal?
4. What kinds of displays might be culturally acceptable, yet at the same time violate more universal ethical principles (e.g., pornography)?

Activity for Extending Thinking

1. Examine the classroom bulletin boards and display areas of several classrooms to determine whether their content contributes to the establishment of a multicultural learning environment. In what ways do displayed materials perpetuate or break down cultural stereotypes?

Presidents of Mount Rushmore: Another Perspective

Several students ask permission to focus their research project on Native American heroes rather than the Mount Rushmore presidents assigned by the teacher.

Ms. Williams was in her third year of teaching, an endeavor that she referred to as "a privilege rather than a job."

She believed deeply in creating and selecting learning activities for students that were based on current events. From a newspaper article on the U.S. government's intention to clean and restore the Mount Rushmore monument (at a cost of $56 million), she designed a group project in which students were to summarize the major accomplishments and admirable traits of a president honored on Mount Rushmore. Ms. Williams thought that the project would not only refine the students' research skills, but it would also give them the opportunity to learn cooperatively.

On the day that she introduced the project to the class, she gave each student a list of the presidents honored on Mount Rushmore: Washington, Jefferson, Lincoln, and Theodore Roosevelt.

After class, Mary Bearrunner and Beth Whiteman, asked Ms. Williams if they could do their project on a Native American chief, such as Crazy Horse. They added that while the presidents on Mount Rushmore had done some good for Whites, each had a hand in what some would call racist acts against Native Americans. "For example," said Beth, "Jefferson bought land from France that actually belonged to Native American people; and he laid the groundwork for 'Manifest Destiny,' which justified taking land and other resources without regard to the rights and cultures of others. And Lincoln approved the mass execution of 38 Indians in Mankato, Minnesota."

Ms. Williams praised the girls for their knowledge of history and responded further, "Here's what I propose."

Questions for Reflection

1. Write the verbatim response you would give to Mary and Beth if you were their teacher.
2. To what extent would you explore with your class the "racist acts" of the presidents? Explain your response.

3. To what extent would the ethnic composition of the class affect your response to question 2?
4. List several other issues related to ethnicity you would want to include in your curriculum. How would you go about including these issues?
5. Is Ms. Williams teaching "heroes history"? Should she have taken a broader ("issues") approach? Which, if any, issues would you include in courses you'll teach?
6. Do young people need heroes in order to develop character and acquire values? Explain.

Activities for Extending Thinking

1. Discuss with three or four students of a variety of ethnic backgrounds how you could better integrate multiethnic content into your curriculum. List the topics and processes that they believe should be included.
2. Discuss with three or four classmates reasons why Mount Rushmore includes the faces of the four presidents it does, and what other presidents, if any, they might think are better selections. Be prepared to share your conclusions in class.

Design Your Own Case

Ethnicity

Based on your personal experience as a statement, or any work in a school as an adult, design a case that explores an issue of ethnicity in the classroom. The story can focus on a method or strategy related to a single subject matter area (e.g., English or social studies) or on a more generic method or strategy pertinent to a wider range of subject matter areas. Your issue might also relate to:

- Planning and preparation
- Classroom environment
- Instruction
- Teacher responsibilities*

Include some demographic data that tell a bit about the community, school, classroom, teacher, students, and curriculum. Include at least one problem for which there is no obvious answer. Use fictitious names of persons and schools to maintain confidentiality.

Your case should be approximately two pages in length (typed, double-spaced) and should include three to four Questions for Reflection and one or two Activities for Extending Thinking. Go to Resource C and use the form to design your own case.

*The four categories are from Danielson, C. (1996). *Enhancing Professional Practice: A Framework for Teaching*. Alexandria, VA: Association for Supervision and Curriculum Development.

Readings for Extending Thinking

Adams, M., Bell, L. A., & Griffin, P. (Eds.). (1997). *Teaching for diversity and social justice: A sourcebook.* New York: Routledge.

Alba, R. D., & Nee, V. (2003). *Remaking the American mainstream: Assimilation and contemporary immigration.* Cambridge, MA: Harvard University Press.

Banks, J. A. (1997). *Teaching strategies for ethnic studies* (6th ed.). Boston: Allyn & Bacon.

Banks, J. A., & Banks, C. A. M. (Eds.). (1995). *Handbook of research on multicultural education.* New York: Macmillan.

Banks, J. A., & Gay, G. (1978). Ethnicity in contemporary American society: Towards the development of a typology. *Ethnicity (5)*, 238–251.

Bialystok, E., & Hakuta, K. (1994). *In other words: The science and psychology of second-language acquisition.* New York: Basic.

Coballes-Vega, C. (1992, January). Considerations for teaching culturally diverse children. *ERIC Digest*, 1–2.

Crawford, J. (1992). *Hold your tongue: Bilingualism and the politics of "English only."* Reading, MA: Addison-Wesley.

Delgado, R., & Stefancic, J. (1997). *Critical white studies: Looking beyond the mirror.* Philadelphia: Temple University Press.

Delpit, L. (1995). *Other people's children: Cultural conflict in the classroom.* New York: Cambridge University Press.

Delpit, L., & Dowdy, J. K. (Eds.). (2002). *The skin that we speak: Thoughts on language and culture in the classroom.* New York: New Press.

Gollnick, D. M., & Chinn, P. C. (2004). *Multicultural education in a pluralistic society: Multimedia edition* (6th ed.). Upper Saddle River, NJ: Merrill/Prentice Hall.

Green, R. L. (2005). *Expectations: How teacher expectations can increase student achievement and assist in closing the achievement gap.* Columbus, OH: SRA/McGraw-Hill.

Henderson, D. L., & May, J. P. (2005). *Exploring culturally diverse literature for children and adolescents: Learning to listen in new ways.* Boston: Pearson Allyn and Bacon.

Hernandez, D. J. (2004). Children and youth in immigrant families. In J. A. Banks & C. A. M. Banks (Eds.), *The handbook of research on multicultural education* (2nd ed., pp. 404–419). San Francisco: Jossey-Bass.

Hollins, E. R., King, J. E., & Hayman, W. C. (Eds.). (1994). *Teaching diverse populations: Formulating a knowledge base.* Albany, NY: State University of New York Press.

Huntington, S. P. (2004). *Who are we? The challenges to America's national identity.* New York: Simon & Schuster.

Irvine, J. J., & York, D. E. (1995). Learning styles and culturally diverse students: A literature review. In J. A. Banks & C. A. M. Banks (Eds.), *The handbook of research on multicultural education* (pp. 484–497). New York: Macmillan.

Jacoby, T. (Ed.). (2004). *Reinventing the melting pot: The new immigrants and what it means to be American.* New York: Basic.

Kailin, J. (1999). How white teachers perceive the problem of racism in the schools: A case study in "liberal" Lakeview. *Teachers College Record, 100,* 724–750.

Kuper, A. (1999). *Culture: The anthropologists' account.* Cambridge, MA: Harvard University Press.

Ladson-Billings, G. (1994). *The dreamkeepers: Successful teachers of African-American children.* San Francisco: Jossey-Bass.

Ladson-Billings, G. (1995). Toward a theory of culturally relevant pedagogy. *American Educational Research Journal, 32,* 465–491.

Manning, M. L., & Baruth, L. G. (1991). Appreciating cultural diversity in the classroom. *Kappa Delta Pi Record, 27*(4), 104–107.

McCall, A. L. (2004). Using poetry in social studies classes to teach about cultural diversity and social justice. *The Social Studies, 95*(4), 172–176.

Perez, B. (1992). Cultural and linguistic democracy: A challenge for today's schools. *Curriculum Report (NASSP), 22*(2), 1–4.

Valdes, G. (2001). *Learning and not learning English: Latino students in American schools.* New York: Teachers College Press.

Wang, M. C., & Gordon, E. W. (Eds.). (1994). *Educational resilience in inner-city America: Challenges and prospects.* Hillsdale, NJ: Lawrence Erlbaum.

Williams, P. J. (1995). *The rooster's egg: On the persistence of prejudice.* Cambridge, MA: Harvard University Press.

Internet Sites for Extending Thinking

http://asianweek.com/news/
News-oriented, current events; profiles Asian stars, other success stories, and analysis of
Asian business trends.

http://www.Indianz.com
Updated news reports on various tribes. Health issues of American Indians, and
contemporary topics.

http://hanksville.org/NAresources
Links to resources on history, culture, art, language, education, and native nations.

http://www.latinolink.com
News, helpful resources in areas such as music and entertainment, business and finance,
sports, education, and careers.

http://www.goshen.edu/soan/rer.htm
Links to race and ethnic relations web sites including groups of european american, african
american, rather native american, and asian american people, as well as to rece and
ethnic relations, cultural competence, and professional organization sites (a web page of
Goshen College Department of Sociology and Anthropology).

Chapter 4

Race

Introduction

Race may be defined as a system of categorization designed to distinguish between groups of persons on the basis of perceived physical differences. This taxonomy, developed over a century ago, has been discredited by more recent studies showing that differences within groups based on physical characteristics are often greater than differences between groups.

For example, groups of color, such as, African-American, Latino, etc., range in skin color from dark brown to white. While most educators today view race as a socially-constructed concept, some teachers, students, and parents hold—perhaps subconsciously—to the age-old view of race, and further, to the view that some "races" are inferior to others (Jacoby & Glauberman, 1995).

Chapter 4 focuses our attention on important issues of race that may be included in the classroom by the teacher or that may arise spontaneously from student impetus. Terms and concepts that often are used or may be useful in discussing the issues of race include:

access	prejudice and discrimination (see Chapter 2
agent group	glossary)
classism	race as a socially constructed concept
equity pedagogy	racism
experiential knowledge	social action activities
institutional racism	student self-esteem
knowledge base	target group
oppression	tracking
power	White privilege

Definitions of key terms are located in the glossary of this text.

Case 11

The Knowledge Base on Diversity: An Aid for Teachers

Recognizing the increasing number of students of diverse racial backgrounds in her school, a teacher explores the knowledge base on racial/ethnic diversity as she makes plans for the coming year.

It was August, and Ms. Johnson was beginning to think seriously about beginning another academic year. She had taught five years, all at Washington School, but had noticed a significant change over the past two years in the demographics of the student body. In fact, the proportion of students of color had increased from 12 percent five years ago to a projected 48 percent for the coming fall.

Ms. Johnson had regularly employed principles for building self-esteem in children and youth, both in her home with her own children, as well as at work with her students. The conceptual framework that she attempted to follow included five principles for building self-esteem in students (Anderson, Redman, & Rogers, 1991):

1. Listen to and acknowledge the thoughts and feelings of students.
2. Structure situations so that they will succeed.
3. Give them reasonable feelings of control over aspects of their lives.
4. Reinforce them for being lovable and capable.
5. Model a positive view of self.

Ms. Johnson was pleased with the results from applying the principles to all her students over the past few years, but with the increasing number of students of color in her school, she wondered if she could be doing more for them—perhaps applying the principles in a slightly different way—to better meet the needs of students of color.

She scanned the table of contents of her favorite resource by Ducette, Sewell, and Shapiro, (1996), "Diversity in Education" edited by Murray, *The Teacher Educators Handbook: Building a Knowledge Base for the Preparation of Teachers,* to get a sense of current research and recommendations for practice. With respect to diversity based on race, she outlined a number of points that seemed to relate to the self-esteem principles with which she was familiar:

1. In studying predominantly working-class Puerto Rican and African-American students, Fine (1989) found that school administrators often censored rather than facilitated the sharing of students' experiences and ideas. For example, racism

was censored so as not to demoralize students, and dropping out of school could not be discussed for it might give students ideas. Conversely, others call for listening to and acknowledging to students and building on their life histories and microcultural experience (Gollnick & Chinn, 1994).

2. Murrell (1995) suggests that in order to structure for success for students of color, we might formulate goals that focus more on experiential knowledge in a social context, particularly as it relates to problems of race, class, gender, and culture (p. 206), and Gollnick and Chinn (1994) intimate that critically analyzing oppression and power relationships will help students understand racism, classism, sexism, and bias against the physically challenged, the young, and the aged.

3. Others suggest that teachers need to discuss crucial decisions made in people's lives, including difficult topics such as drug use, having a baby, and dropping out of school (Aronowitz & Giroux, 1985).

4. The same authors suggest engaging students in collective social action to ensure a democratic society (Gollnick & Chinn, 1994). Others suggest sublimating traditional individualistic reward systems in favor of goals for the collective advancement of the racial/ethnic community at hand (Fordham, 1988). Such rewards may more effectively reinforce students of color as lovable and capable.

5. In a study of urban, working-class students, it was found that a group of white students who believed that school would not lead to success were found to be using wealthy, not-well-educated persons in the community as role models (MacLeod, 1987). Perhaps providing more appropriate (e.g., more educated, less wealthy) models would benefit such students.

In previous years of teaching, Ms. Johnson had based her curriculum and instruction on research, theory, and "best practice." As she reviewed her outline of accepted studies on racial/ethnic diversity, she began to envision ways of converting theory to practice in her own classroom. It would again be exciting to try some new ideas, this time with a new and more diverse group of students.

Question for Reflection

1. Design an outline of a unit plan in your own subject matter area. For example, a unit on racism might begin:

Students will better understand the central nature, cause, concept, and effects of racism (objective), and use a mapping strategy to identify prior knowledge of the nature, cause, and effects of this form of bias (activity). You might decide that assessment of this activity will be based on performance on a project as measured by a rubric specifying criteria.

The Unit description might be followed by 8 to 10 lesson plans that would form a general, rough draft outline of a teaching unit based on the concept of racism and related issues.

Objective	Activity	Assessment Strategy
a.		
b.		
c.		
d.		
e.		

2. Design a plan for implementing one of the research findings on pages 45 & 46, in classes you will likely teach. In 1 to 2 pages, include a general goal (or goals), a key strategy or two for addressing the goal (s) and a general statement about how you will assess outcomes.

Activity for Extending Thinking

1. How could you translate theory to practice for each of the research-based ideas previously noted? From each of the studies previously outlined, list at least one practical strategy that you could employ in your own teaching to address those findings. Identify the grade level and subject matter area for which you intend the curriculum or instructional plan.

Objective	Activity	Assessment Strategy
a.		
b.		
c.		
d.		
e.		

Case 12

Students Right an Injustice

*Students extend and refine reading and writing skills
as they engage in a "social action" activity.*

Mr. Hultgren's class had been keeping a record of upcoming class events such as field trips, students report days, and quizzes on a commercial calendar. The pictures on the calendar were of children and adolescents—mostly close-ups showing facial expressions such as wonder, excitement, happiness, and awe. On the first day of November, Mr. Hultgren turned the page of the calendar. Hector, an outgoing youth of Mexican heritage, asked his teacher, "Mr. Hultgren, how come none of the pictures on the calendar have any kids that look like me?" Other students of color chimed in, "Yeah, or me?"

Mr. Hultgren had not paid much attention to the pictures on the calendar. "You're right," he replied, looking through the rest of the pages. "There are no children of color in the remaining pictures, either. Can anyone think of anything we could do about this?"

Marty offered a suggestion, "Perhaps we can write to the people who made the calendar and ask them to put in pictures of kids like us in their next one." The class agreed.

Mr. Hultgren briefly explained about calendar publishing companies and how they could find out to whom they should write. He then designed some activities that included prewriting, editing, rewriting, spelling, grammar and usage, and business letter format. For the next week, students devised, edited, and revised a class letter to the calendar company. The letter was sent on Friday.

Five weeks later, the class received a letter from the calendar company. It said, "Thank you for making us aware of this oversight. We apologize for our mistake and we plan to add students of color to the calendar next year."

Questions for Reflection

1. What were the strengths of Mr. Hultgren's response to the calendar problem? What else would you have said and done if you had been in his position?
2. List the specific behaviors of Mr. Hultgren that likely
   a. demonstrated teacher and student efficacy;
   b. created an inclusive classroom environment;
   c. enhanced learning of academic material.

3. Describe any experiences you have had in which students have taken a social-action approach to solve a real problem in the school or broader community (see "Social Action Approach" in the Banks model, Resource B).
4. How could you design an activity that would encourage pupils to discuss the Banks model and to identify social-action issues that they could address? How could you ensure that such a discussion was developmentally appropriate?

Activity for Extending Thinking

1. Discuss with practicing teachers, students, and parents the social problems and issues that could/should be addressed in the kinds of classes you teach or will teach. For each social problem or issue listed, identify one or two activities that would encourage students to gather relevant data, examine their own values and those of others, and take thoughtful actions to help resolve the problem or issue. (See examples in Resource B, "Social Action Approach.")

13

Use of the N-Word in the Classroom

A teacher considers how to respond to four male friends—three
African-American and one White—who use the term "nigga"
as a term of endearment in her classroom.

Daunte, Denzel, Michael, and Ryan had been inseparable over the past year. They had first become friends through working in small groups in one of their classes and had strengthened the bond of friendship as football buddies and in just "hanging out" after school, enjoying rap music. Most of all they seemed to enjoy having fun giving and taunting one another with friendly quips designed to both show their wit and to affirm their friendship.

Daunte, Denzel, and Michael were of African-American descent; Ryan was White. Often, taunts related to the ancestry of the four friends. "Hey, my nigga" was a greeting often extended by and to the African-American friends; "Hey, my wigga" (the abbreviation for white nigga) was a common greeting for Ryan. For classmates who knew of their close and long-lived relationship, this form of language seemed clearly inclusive and affirming, especially when used in the informal contexts of the neighborhood and the school hallways.

However, their teacher, Ms. Persons, was new to the school and had no knowledge of the friendship of the four. Her first introduction to their jiving and taunting of one another came toward the end of the morning as the class geared down to get ready for lunch. As students put their papers and books in their bags, Ms. Persons overheard what the four friends thought was a private conversation. She also was sure that several other students overheard them as they gathered to walk together:

"What it is, my nigga?" Ryan asked Denzel.

"Hey, wigga," Denzel replied.

As Daunte approached the two, Ryan smiled. "Yo, bro. I starved—let's go eat."

Ms. Persons' ears had begun to burn after the first greeting. Her first thought was that such language should never be tolerated in any classroom. At the same time, the boys did seem to be friendly toward one another; it was obvious that the interaction was not intended to harm. Yet what about the other students who had heard the exchange? Would ignoring the exchange give permission to others in the class to use such terms?

She didn't need this challenge on the first day of class, for she knew that it could have a significant effect on the development of respect and rapport between her and the class and among the students. Knowing she had but a few short moments to respond, she wondered what, if anything, she would say.

Questions for Reflection

1. What would you say (verbatim) to the boys?
2. If you thought that because the terms "nigga" and "wigga" were in common use in the school and hence may be used again in your classroom, and if you therefore decided it might be best to discuss the implications of the use of such terms with your class, outline the questions that you would want to ask and the points that you would want to make in the class discussion.
   a. Questions:
   b. Points to be made:
3. What rationale would you use to explain to others (your class, parents of your students, colleagues) your decision to discuss the issue in class?
4. Is it appropriate for a White student who is referred to as a "wigga" by a close of color to refer to his friend of color as a "nigga"? Why or why not? Is it ever appropriate for a White teacher to use the "er" version of the N – word? Why or why not?
5. What other racial epithets might warrant discussion with your classes? List as many such terms as you can.

Activities for Extending Thinking

1. Review current resources on the pros and cons of deconstructing racial epithets such as the N – word. Summarize the key insights you obtain from the readings.
2. Interview two teachers in urban schools who have had encounters such as the one in the story. Summarize their opinions on the issue of responding to the student use of such terms.
3. Interview White students and students of color who have attended urban schools with diverse student populations. Ask them about their views on the use of terms that are sometimes used as terms of inclusivity and at other times as racial epithets. Summarize your findings in writing.
4. Knowing that your students may inadvertently encounter Web sites or print materials that use racial epithets, what preventative measures, if any, would you take to mitigate against such encounters? Would you purposely direct students to such sites in order that they might formulate ways to counter the effects of the negative messages? Why or why not?

14

Hey, Teach—You Trippin' on Me, but Not on the White Kids!

A teacher is accused of racist behavior by a student in her class.

It was Friday, the sixth week of school, and the day of the big game with the rival school. Excitement was in the air. Ms. Moss's students were caught up in the spirit of the moment as they entered her room, talking and laughing with each other. Ms. Moss liked this class and was pleased about the mutual respect that existed between her and the vast majority of her students.

The bell rang. Ms. Moss and her students had discussed and followed a clear routine for beginning class. It was understood that they had four minutes to complete their conversations, take their seats and assemble their books, and papers.

Those first four minutes of free time for the students also allowed Ms. Moss to complete attendance and to sign passes for students who were tardy or absent the previous day.

"Okay, class, it's time to begin," she said.

This day, the students were not as responsive as they usually had been in the past. Their conversations trailed on. Several students had not yet taken their seats. "Marty, Willie, Desweon, please, sit down."

When students did not respond, Ms. Moss moved toward the students who seemed to be loudest and least responsive. Her intent was to use proximity—a closer and more personal presence—to get the students' attention.

She spoke more loudly to be sure she was heard. "Desweon, Willie, I asked you to please sit down. It's time to start class."

Desweon turned to Ms. Moss. "Why you be trippin' on us? You didn't say anything to those guys," pointing to three White students across the room. "You trippin' on us' cause we're Black!"

"I'm trippin' on you because you're the loudest and the closest. I'm on my way to say the same thing to Marty and Tom. Now you sit down, please." Ms. Moss paused just long enough for a response, and then continued toward the White students, somewhat surprised and disappointed that she had been accused of being racist.

With personal directives to the most talkative and loudest, the class began to settle down. Ms. Moss thought to herself, "What other follow-up would be appropriate? Should I talk to Desweon and Willie in the hall? Should I discuss the incident with the class? Do I need other information about the students who were involved?" She decided to think about it overnight.

That evening as she pondered the questions from the incident that day, she also wondered about other details: Could there have been some underlying negative racial attitudes that affected her response to the class? Why didn't she approach the White students first? She had always tried to be an advocate for students of traditionally oppressed groups; she even voluntarily served as chair of the text-bias review committee for the district. Perhaps even a culturally sensitive teacher could be unknowingly influenced by some underlying attitudes. She began to think about other recent reprimands for indicators of patterns.

Questions for Reflection

1. Assess Ms. Moss's behavior in class. What behaviors, if any, were appropriate? Which, if any, were inappropriate?
2. What else, if anything, would you have done at the time of the confrontation by Desweon?
3. What, if anything, would you do as a follow-up, later that day or in the following days?
4. What local, state, and/or national standards for teacher education relate to the key issues in this case?
5. In light of increased backlash to acts of terrorism (backlash in the form of violence and other forms of discrimination), outline several steps you could take as a teacher to counter negative student attitudes towards persons perceived as being of Middle Eastern decent.

Activities for Extending Thinking

1. Develop a prevention plan that would minimize the likelihood of being accused of being racist by a student or students.
2. In a school setting—a field experience site or arranged visit—discuss the issue (teacher accused of racism by student) with a teacher and student of color, and with a White teacher and student. Record their suggestions for avoiding and for responding to such an accusation.
3. Discuss with colleagues in your teacher preparation program incidents similar to the one above. Record their recommendations for preventing and for responding to this issue.
4. With peers or professional educators, discuss how a teacher might respond if accused by a student of being sexist or biased in terms of socioeconomic status, ethnicity, religion, language, special needs, or sexual orientation.

A Lesson on Oppression and Whiteness

White students ask "What's in it for me?" and struggle to identify
social group membership in a lesson on social oppression.

For several years Mr. Albornoz had taught children in the early elementary grades. Each year he had taught about discrimination in a concrete way—by replicating the "Blue Eyes/Brown Eyes" activity developed by Jane Eliot. On the first day of this simulation, blue-eyed students were considered "superior," and were given privileges such as extra servings at the cafeteria, use of the drinking fountain, and extra time at recess. On the second day, roles were reversed so that all students could experience feelings related to being treated as inferior as well as superior.

In follow-up discussions of feelings of pupils in the superior and inferior groups, it was clear that they were not ready to discuss the plight of another group, such as African-Americans or gays, without first having talked about their own ethnic group. When he brought up group names like Native American, Latino, Asian, or African-American, the White pupils would consistently ask, "What about us?"

With this question in mind, and working this year with older students, Mr. Albornoz sought new ways to begin his lessons on social oppression. He had been impressed with the Oppression Model in a text entitled *Teaching for Diversity and Social Justice* (1997). The model is based on helping students identify their own social group membership (gender, class, sexual orientation, physical/developmental/psychological ability, race, religion, and age), and then applying that information. The Oppression Model lists forms of oppression, e.g., racism, the agent group in that form, e.g., Whites, and the target groups of that form of oppression, e.g., Blacks, Latinos, Asians, Native Americans, biracial people. Other forms of oppression were sexism, classism, ageism, and bias toward religion, ethnicity, persons of gay/lesbian/bisexual/transsexual (GLBT) orientation, and persons with disabilities. Students are then asked a series of questions related to ease of identifying their status (agent or target) for each group membership. In pairs, students answer questions such as: which group membership(s) were easiest to identify as your own, were hardest to identify as your own, were you least aware of, and would you like to know more about?

On this day, as students began to examine their own social group membership, and more specifically their own ethnicity, Jeremy, a White student of upper-middle economic class parents, stated: "Hey Mr. A., I'm an American; that's my group!" Other White students nodded in agreement. "All White people are American." Mr. Albornoz replied: "Are others in class—our African-American and Latino brothers and sisters—not American?" Jeremy appeared puzzled.

The teacher continued: "And is 'American' an ethnic group?"

Luis responded: "No, I think 'American' is a term that refers to a national group."

"That's right," replied Mr. Albornoz. "It is indeed."

Marie offered her thoughts: "Everyone has an ethnic background—that is, they share a common culture that distinguishes them from other groups, like German or Italian-Americans. They have traditions common to their group, but traditions that are different from other groups."

"Very good!" replied Mr. Albornoz. Turning to Jeremy, he continued: "So Jeremy, what ethnic group or groups do you think are part of your heritage?"

Jeremy thought: "Well, I guess my mother is Swedish and my father is German and maybe English."

"So if those are your ethnic groups, of what other social groups are you a member?" pressed Mr. Albornoz. "Write them down on your paper—I'll collect them in a few minutes."

Realizing that some students may not know their ethnic heritage, Mr. Albornoz instructed them to write "unknown," until they could talk to their parents. After allowing a couple of minutes for students to write their ethnic and other social groups on their papers, Mr. Albornoz posed a new question. "Looking at our Oppression Model, to which agent (oppressive) groups and which target (oppressed) groups do you belong? Write them down on the same paper." Tomorrow, when he returned the papers, Mr. Albornoz would ask them about stereotypes often assigned to target groups, as well as how members of each agent and target group might interact with a member of another group.

"Can we be a member of both agent and target groups?" asked Kim.

"Yes, most of us are," replied the teacher. "Now," he continued, "what privileges or advantages do people in any of the agent groups have over persons in a target group?"

"What do you mean?" asked one of the students.

"Take for example, those of us who are White—do we have any advantages over persons of color—just because of our skin color?"

"Yeah," stated Will, "We Whites don't get harassed with racial profiling—you know, arrested for 'DWB, driving while Black.' "

"And we are less likely to be closely watched for shoplifting in stores," added another White student.

"Ok, in your pairs, list a couple of advantages possessed by each agent group, like males, upper-middle economic class people, heterosexuals, gentiles or Christians, nondisabled persons, and young and middle-aged adults," said Mr. Albornoz.

As the students discussed in pairs, Mr. Albornoz thought about how he would debrief student comments, and help students distinguish between forms of oppression—individual, institutional, and societal—and related issues.

Questions for Reflection

1. If some of your students could not recognize the difference between being White and being American, what questions, metaphors, and other techniques could you use to help them differentiate the two?
2. What forms of "White privilege" have you personally observed?
3. How could you teach a similar lesson (on oppression or Whiteness) in your own subject matter area, i.e., in what course and unit could you include it? How would you tie it to your course and unit in your introduction of the lesson?

Activity for Extending Thinking

1. Examine a model of White racial-identity theory (e.g., Helms, 1995) and one of racial identity theory of persons of color (e.g., Hardiman & Jackson, 1992; Helms, 1995; Tatum, 1997). Apply the developmental stages to your current status, i.e., identify the stage that you feel best matches your attitudes and beliefs.

Design Your Own Case

Race

Design a case that explores an issue of race in the classroom. The story can focus on a method or strategy related to a single subject matter area (e.g., English or social studies) or on a more generic method or strategy pertinent to a wider range of subject matter areas. Your issue might also relate to:

- Planning and preparation
- Classroom environment
- Instruction
- Teacher responsibilities*

In selecting a topic, reflect on recent or current field experiences, personal experiences as a student, or accounts of real classroom incidents. Include some demographic data that tell a bit about the community, school, classroom, teacher, students, and curriculum. Include at least one problem to which there is no obvious answer. Use fictitious names of persons and schools to maintain confidentiality.

Your case should be approximately two pages in length (typed, double-spaced) and should include three to four Questions for Reflection, and one or two Activities for Extending Thinking. Go to Resource C and use the form to design your own case.

---

*The four categories are from *Enhancing Professional Practice: A Framework for Teaching*, by C. Danielson, 1996. Alexandria, VA: Association for Supervision and Curriculum Development.

Readings for Extending Thinking

Anderson, E. M., Redman, G. L., & Rogers, C. (1991). Self-esteem for tots to teens. 1480 Arden View Drive, Arden Hills, MN 55112: Parenting and Teaching for Self-Esteem.

Apple, M. W. (1997). Consuming the other: Whiteness, education, and cheap french fries. In M. Fine, L. Weis, L. Powell, & L. Wang (Eds.), *Off White: Readings on race, power, and society* (pp. 121–128). New York: Routledge.

Aronowitz, S., & Giroux, H. A. (1985). *Education under siege*. Westport, CT: Bergin & Garvey.

Asante, M. K. (1991–1992). Afrocentric curriculum. *Educational Leadership, 49*(4), 28–31.

Bock, M., Rendon, M., & Kellogg, P. (2000). *Whiteness at work: A positive diversity curriculum*. Minneapolis, MN: Sirius Communications.

Brown, D. L. (1999, January 13). No easy lessons on race: Black parents find new ways to prepare children. *The Washington Post*, p. A-1.

Bush, L. (1996). "The N Word." *New Yorker, 72*(10), 50.

Clark, C., & O'Donnell, J. (Eds.). (1999). *Becoming and unbecoming White: Owning and disowning a racial identity*. Westport, CT: Greenwood Press.

Council of Economic Advisors. (1998, September). *Changing America: Indicators of social and economic well-being by race and Hispanic origin*. Washington, DC: United States Government Printing Office.

Cushner, M., McClelland, A., & Safford, P. (1992). *Human diversity in education: An integrative approach*. New York: McGraw-Hill.

Darling-Hammond, L. (1998, September). Unequal opportunity: Race and education. *Brookings Review,* 28–32.

Delpit, L. (1995). *Other people's children: Cultural conflict in the classroom*. New York: New Press.

Deyhle, D., & Swisher, K. (1997). Research in American Indian and Alaska Native education: From assimilation to self-determination. In M. W. Apple (Ed.), *Review of research in education* (Vol. 22, pp. 113–194). Washington, DC: American Educational Research Association.

Dovidio, J. F., & Gaertner, S. L. (1998). On the nature of contemporary prejudice: The causes, consequences, and challenges of aversive racism. In J. L. Eberhardt & S. T. Fiske (Eds.), *Confronting racism: The problem and the response* (pp. 3–32). Thousand Oaks, CA: Sage.

Ducette, J., Sewell, T., & Shapiro, J. (1996). Diversity in education. In F. B. Murray (Ed.), *The teacher educators handbook: Building a knowledge base for the preparation of teachers* (pp. 323–380). San Francisco: Jossey-Bass.

Dunn, R., Gemake, J., Jalali, F., & Zenhausern, R. (1990). Cross-cultural differences in learning styles of elementary-age students from four ethnic backgrounds. *Journal of Multicultural Counseling and Development, 18,* 68–93.

Dupree, D., Spencer, M. B., & Bell, S. (1997). The ecology of African-American child development: Normative and non-normative outcomes. In G. Johnson-Powell, J. Yamamoto, G. E. Wyatt, & W. Arroyo (Eds.), *Transcultural child development: Psychological assessment and treatment* (pp. 237–268). New York: Wiley.

Fine, M. (1989). Silencing and nurturing voice in an improbable context: Urban adolescents in public school. In H. A. Giroux & P. McLaren (Eds.), *Critical pedagogy, the state and cultural struggle.* Albany, NY: State University of New York Press.

Fine, M. (1991). *Framing dropouts: Notes on the politics of urban high schools.* Albany, NY: State University of New York Press.

Fordham, S. (1988). Racelessness as a factor in Black students' school success: Pragmatic strategy or pyrrhic victory. *Harvard Educational Review, 58,* 54–84.

Foster, M. (1991). "Just got to find a way": Case studies of the lives and practice of exemplary black high school teachers. In M. Foster (Ed.), *Into schools and schooling.* New York: AMS Press.

Foster, M. (1997). *Black teachers on teaching.* New York: New Press.

Garibaldi, A. M. (1986). Sustaining Black educational progress: Challenges for the 1990s. *Journal of Negro Education, 55*(3), 386–396.

Gibbs, J. T. (1988). *Young, Black and male in America: An endangered species.* Dover, DE: Auburn House.

Gollnick, D. M., & Chinn, P. C. (1994). Multicultural education in a pluralistic society. (4th ed.). Upper Saddle River, NJ: Merrill/Prentice Hall.

Grant, C. A., & Secada, W. G. (1991). Preparing teachers for diversity. In W. R. Houston (Ed.), *Handbook of research on teacher education.* New York: Macmillan.

Hale-Benson, J. E. (1982). *Black children: Their roots, culture, and learning style.* Baltimore: Johns Hopkins University Press.

Hardiman, R., & Jackson, B. W. (1992). Racial identity development: Understanding racial dynamics in college classroom and on campus. In M. Adams (Ed.), (1997) *Promoting diversity in college classrooms: Innovative responses for the curriculum, faculty and institutions* (pp. 21–37). San Francisco: Jossey-Bass.

Harvey, K. D., & Harjo, L. D. (1994). *Indian country: A history of native people in America.* Golden, CO: North American Press.

Helms, J. E. (1995). An update of Helms' White and people of color racial identity models. In J. P. Ponterotto, J. M. Casas, L. A. Suzuki, & C. M. Alexander (Eds.), *Handbook of multicultural counseling* (pp. 181–198). Thousand Oaks, CA: Sage.

Jacoby, R., & Glauberman, N. (1995). *The bell curve debate: History, documents, opinions.* New York: Times Books.

Joe, J. R. (1994). Revaluing Native American concepts of development and education. In P.M. Greenfield & R. R. Cocking (Eds.), *Cross-cultural roots of minority child development* (pp. 107–113). Hillsdale, NJ: Lawrence Erlbaum.

Kennedy, R. (2002). *Nigger: The strange career of a troublesome word.* New York: Pantheon.

Kivel, P. (1996). *Uprooting racism: How White people can work for racial justice.* Philadelphia: New Society.

Levin, S. (2000). Social psychological evidence on race and racism. In M. Chang, D. Witt, J. Jones, & K. Hakuta (Eds.), *Compelling interest: Examining the evidence on racial dynamics in higher education.* Stanford, CA: Stanford University Press.

MacLeod, J. (1987). *Ain't no makin' it: Leveled aspirations in a low-income neighborhood.* Boulder, CO: Westview Press.

Montagu, A. (1997). *Race, man's most dangerous myth: The fallacy of race.* Walnut Creek, CA: Altamira Press (Original work published 1942).

Murrell, P. C. (1995). What is missing in the preparation of minority teachers? In M. Foster (Ed.), *Into schools and schooling.* New York: AMS Press.

NAACP activists upset over dictionary's definition of the word "nigger." *Jet, 91*(3), 23–24.

The NAEP 1998 reading report card: National & state highlights. (1999). Washington, DC: Office of Educational Research and Improvement, U.S. Department of Education.

Novick, M. (1995). *White lies, White power: The fight against White supremacy and reactionary violence.* Monroe, ME: Common Courage Press.

Orfield, G., & Yun, J. T. (1999). *Resegregation in American schools.* Cambridge, MA: The Civil Rights Project, Harvard University.

Phillips, M., Brooks-Gunn, J., Duncan, G. J., Klebanov, P., & Crane, J. (1998a). Family background, parenting practices, and the Black-White test score gap. In C. Jencks & M. Phillips (Eds.), *The Black-White test score gap.* Washington, DC: Brookings Institution Press.

Phillips, M. et al. (1998b). Does the Black-White test score gap widen after children enter school? In C. Jencks & M. Phillips (Eds.), *The Black-White test score gap.* Washington, DC: Brookings Institutional Press.

Rasool, J. A., & Curtis, A. C. (2000). *Multicultural education in the middle and secondary classrooms: Meeting the challenge of diversity and change.* Belmont, CA: Wadsworth/Thomson Learning.

Robinson-Zañartu, C. (1996, October). Serving Native American children and families: Considering cultural variables. *Language, speech, and hearing services in schools, 27*(4), 373–384.

School superintendent in Nevada under fire for using the word "nigger." (2000, August 28). *Jet, 98*(12), 18.

Shade, B. J. (1989). *Culture and learning style within the Afro-American community.* New York: Stone.

Solorzano, D. G. (1998). Critical race theory, race and gender microaggressions, and the experience of Chicana and Chicano students. *International Journal of Qualitative Studies in Education, 11,* 121–137.

Steele, C. M., & Aronson, J. (1995). Stereotype threat and the intellectual test performance of African Americans. *Journal of Personality and Social Psychology, 69,* 797–811.

Tatum, B. D. (1997). *"Why are all the Black kids sitting together in the cafeteria?" And other conversations about race.* New York: Basic.

Tatum, W. F., IV. (1997). Critical race theory and education: History, theory, and implications. In M. Apple (Ed.), *Review of research in education* (pp. 195–250). Washington, DC: American Educational Research Association.

Watkins, W. H., Lewis, J. H., & Chou, V. (2001). *Race and education.* Boston: Allyn & Bacon.

Watson, D. C. (2001, Spring). Deconstructing the "N" word. *The Hamline Review,* 51–61.

Wellman, D. (1999). Transforming received categories: Discovering cross-border identities and other subversive activities. In C. Clark & J. O'Donnell (Eds.), *Becoming and unbecoming White: Owning and disowning a racial identity* (pp. 78–91). Westport, CT: Greenwood Press.

Wijeyesinghe, C. L., and Jackson, B. W., III. (2001). *New perspectives on racial identity development: A theoretical and practical anthology.* New York: New York University Press.

Wing, A. K. (Ed.). (1997). *Critical race feminism: A reader.* New York: University Press.

Zirkel, P. A. (1999). The "N" word. *Phi Delta Kappan, 80*(9), 713–715.

African-Americans

Baker, L. D. (1998). *From savage to Negro: Anthropology and the construction of race: 1896–1954.* Berkeley, CA: University of California.

Egerton, J. (1994). *Speak now against the day: The generation before the civil rights movement in the South.* New York: Knopf.

Frisby, C. L. (1993). One giant step backward: Myths of Black cultural learning styles. *School Psychology Review, 22,* 535–557.

Igus, T. (Ed.). (1991). *Book of Black heroes: Great women in the struggle.* New York: Scholastic.

Jarrett, R. L. (1995). Growing up poor: The family experience of socially mobile youth in low-income African American neighborhoods. *Journal of Adolescent Research, 10*(1), 111–135.

Magill, F. N. (Ed.). (1992). *Masterpieces of African American literature.* New York: HarperCollins.

Southern Poverty Law Center. (1989). *Free at last: A history of the civil rights movement and those who died in the struggle.* Montgomery, AL: Teaching Tolerance.

Srickland, D. S. (1994). Educating African American learners at risk: Finding a better way. *Language Arts, 71,* 328–336.

Native Americans

Brown, D. (1970). *Bury my heart at Wounded Knee: An Indian history of the American West.* New York: Henry Holt.

Deyhle, D., & LeCompte, M. (1994). Cultural differences in child development: Navajo adolescents in middle schools. *Theory Into Practice, 33,* 156–167.

Jaimes, A. (1992). *The state of Native America: Genocide, colonization, and resistance.* Boston: South End Press.

Kast, S. (1993–1994). Mobilizing and empowering Native American youth. *Children Today, 22*(2), 27–31.

Nel, J. (1994). Preventing school failure: The Native American child. *The Clearing House, 67,* 169–174.

Reyhner, J. (1994). American Indian/Alaska Native education. (Phi Delta Kappa Fastback 367). Bloomington, IN: Phi Delta Kappa.

Riley, P. (Ed.). (1993). *Growing up Native American: An anthology.* New York: Morrow.

Shaffer, D. D. (1993). Making Native American lessons meaningful. *Childhood Education, 69,* 201–203.

Weatherford, J. (1991). *Native roots: How the Indians enriched America.* New York: Crown.

Asian-Americans

Chan, S. (1994). *Hmong means free: Life in Laos and America.* Philadelphia: Temple University Press.

Chong, D. (1994). *The concubine's children: The story of a Chinese family living on two sides of the globe.* New York: Penguin.

Donnelly, N. D. (1994). *Changing lives of refugee Hmong women.* Seattle, WA: University of Washington Press.

Feng, J. (1994, June). *Asian-American children: What teachers should know.* ERIC Digest, 1–2.

Hamanaki, S. (1990). *The journey: Japanese Americans, racism, and renewal.* New York: Orchard.

Hong, M. (Ed.). (1993). *Growing up Asian American.* New York: Avon.

Okihiro, G. Y. (1994). *Margins and mainstreams: Asians in American history and culture.* Seattle, WA: University of Washington Press.

Salyer, L. E. (1995). *Laws harsh as tigers: Chinese immigrants and the shaping of modern immigration law.* Chapel Hill, NC: University of North Carolina Press.

Siu, S. F. (1994). *Taking no chances: Profile of a Chinese-American family's support for school success.* Boston: Wheelock College.

Takaki, R. (1989). *Strangers from a different shore: A history of Asian Americans.* Boston: Little, Brown.

Trask, H. K. (1993). *From a native daughter: Colonialism & sovereignty in Hawaii.* Monroe, ME: Common Courage Press.

Yen, C. C., & Lee, S. N. (1994). Applicability of the learning style inventory in an Asian context and its predictive value. *Educational and Psychological Measurement, 54,* 541–549.

Hispanic/Latina(o)s

Augenbraum, H., & Stavans, I. (Eds.). (1993). *Growing up Latino: Memoirs and stories.* Boston: Houghton Mifflin.

Carlson, L. M. (Ed.). (1994). *Cool salsa: Bilingual poems on growing up Latino in the United States.* New York: Henry Holt.

Casteneda, D. M. (1994). A research agenda for Mexican American adolescent mental health. *Adolescence, 29,* 225–239.

Cofer, J. O. (1990). *Silent dancing: A partial remembrance of a Puerto Rican childhood.* Houston, TX: Arte Publico Press.

Jimenez, C. M. (1994). *The Mexican American heritage* (2nd ed., rev. and expanded). Berkeley, CA: TQS Publications.

Kanellos, N. (1994). *The Hispanic almanac: From Columbus to corporate America.* Detroit, MI: Visible Ink Press.

Marcell, A. V. (1994). Understanding ethnicity, identity formation, and risk behavior among adolescents of Mexican descent. *Journal of School Health, 64,* 323–327.

Mendoza, J. I. (1994). On being a Mexican American. *Phi Delta Kappan, 76,* 293–295.

Muñoz, V. I. (1995). *Where something catches: Work, love, and identity in youth.* Albany, NY: State University of New York Press.

Internet Sites for Extending Thinking

http://eddept.wa.edu.au/abled/antiracism.html
Lists URLs and descriptions of numerous major international sites on antiracism.

http://library.csus.edu/guides/kochism/diversity/div_web.htm
Contains websites and directions on diverse populations, including Africans, Asians,
indigenous populations, Latin Americans and Middle Easterners as well as women,
GLBT, ability groups and aging populations.

http://curry.edschool.virginia.edu/go/multicultural/papers/shin.html
Personal narrative of a teacher on color, color blindness, and education.

http://www.altavista.com
Type "african American webliography" in the "Web Page Search" box and click on
"Search."

Chapter 5

Socioeconomic Status

Introduction

Socioeconomic status (S.E.S) is a concept that includes one's educational attainment, occupation, and income (U.S. Census Bureau, 1999). Students often rank one another on these factors, resulting in a hierarchy that rewards some, and demeans others. Low rankings often result in lower feelings of self-regard, reduced motivation to achieve, and concomitant negative attitudes toward schools, teachers, classmates, and society.

Furthermore, teachers need to know how to help our future citizens understand economic and political proposals that differentially affect various socioeconomic groups. "Understanding how social and economic class operates in the United States is important in order for them to be able to participate in these debates in an informed way" (Adams, et al., 1997).

Chapter 5 contains cases that deal with socioeconomic issues that often result in differential and unfair treatment of students. Discussion of the cases in this section often include references to terms and phrases such as:

assessment criteria	free and reduced-price lunch programs
behavior modification	high-poverty school
effects of childrearing practices	poverty
emotional literacy	S.E.S.
establishing incentives	

Definitions of key terms are located in the glossary of this text.

Case 16

A New Student and a Lesson in Geography

An experience with a new student reminds a teacher to use caution in relating socioeconomic status to outward appearance.

As are most teachers, Mr. McDonald was dedicated and creative, and he cared about his students. Teaching was his passion. Nearly all the students in his class lived in the economically deprived neighborhood in which the school was located. Only about 15 percent of the student body were of middle-class means. It was the sixth week of school when Peter, an African-American transfer student from Chicago, entered his class. Peter was dressed like the other students, with a T-shirt and worn blue jeans. Mr. McDonald welcomed Peter into the class and gave him the usual materials: a text, handouts related to the current unit, and a set of free lunch tickets for the remainder of the week.

"Any questions?" asked Mr. McDonald.

"Yeah," Peter said. "What am I supposed to do with these tickets?"

"Just give them to the woman at the cash register in the lunchroom," replied Mr. McDonald. He then began his lesson on European history. Later in the hour, when he was well into his lesson, Mr. McDonald asked, "Can anyone tell me if one could get to Europe via the North Sea?" Peter quickly shot his hand into the air with confidence. "Yes. Actually I've crossed the North Sea by boat with my family."

Doubting that Peter had ever made such a trip, Mr. McDonald replied, "You're right, Peter: It is possible to reach Europe by the North Sea." As the hour was coming to an end, Mr. McDonald reminded students of the homework for the next day. Just as the dismissal bell rang, he finished giving the assignments.

On his way out of the room, Peter asked Mr. McDonald where he should go to get a bus pass. Mr. McDonald informed Peter that he would not need one—that all the kids walked home. Peter glanced quizzically at his new teacher and then was swallowed by the stream of students.

When Mr. McDonald made his usual stop in the principal's office the next morning to get his announcements and messages, the school secretary reminded him to have Peter pick up his bus pass. Mr. McDonald admitted that he had told Peter to walk home the day before. "Five miles!?" asked the secretary. "You know he lives in Roseville [a middle-class suburb], don't you?"

Mr. McDonald admitted that he had not known that Peter's family lived in the neighboring middle-class community. "That explains Peter's puzzled look when I handed him the free lunch tickets," he thought. Mr. McDonald wondered what he would say to Peter later that day in class.

Questions for Reflection

1. What were Mr. McDonald's assumptions about Peter, and on what did he base them?
2. In your experience as a student, what assumptions have teachers made about you because of your socioeconomic status? About others in your P-12 classes?
3. What can teachers do to prevent/counter the negative effects of student bias based on socio-economic status?
4. What kind of background information should teachers obtain about their new students to avoid the kinds of problems in this story? Where possible, should teachers use student files to learn about them? When no background information is available, how can teachers avoid making assumptions?
5. How could you help students in your classes understand the importance of getting to know another person rather than making assumptions based on prejudgments?

Activities for Extending Thinking

1. Talk individually with at least two students of a different socioeconomic background (avoid making assumptions when selecting your students). If you plan to use students from a field-experience placement, be sure to inform your cooperating teacher of your plans. Discuss with each student his or her likes and dislikes with respect to out-of-class activities (e.g., hobbies, sports, pets), as well as in-class preferences for learning. Be prepared to share insights.
2. Review one research-based resource from the "Readings for Extending Thinking" at the end of this chapter or from another text (e.g., a primary course text) that would add to your knowledge about the effects of socioeconomic status on students with whom you work. Summarize key insights in writing, and be prepared to share in class.
3. Discuss with a school administrator or counselor the teaching/learning, human development, legal and/or human-relationship competencies needed by teachers who work with students of various socioeconomic backgrounds.
4. Design a plan for a classroom school essay contest with a theme of personal experience with either (a) being the target of discrimination or (b) being successful in confronting some form of bias. Negotiate to have the winning entries published in the school and community newspaper.

Case | 17

Gangs and the Victims of Violence— Writing as a Therapy

Students from an economically deprived neighborhood are given a writing assignment in which they express their feelings about the hurtful effects of gang activity.

Ms. Soltow knew her students well. She was fully aware that many of her students were from homes ravaged by crime and poverty. Gang activity was commonplace. Many students had one parent at home—in most cases, a mother. Many of her students had to work at home—baby-sitting, for example—to help their working parent or parents. A number of the students had lost friends or relatives to homicide.

It was week four of school, and as usual Ms. Soltow had established a healthy rapport with her students. In an attempt to address some of their emotional needs, and at the same time to provide an opportunity for them to develop their writing abilities, Ms. Soltow addressed the class: "Often in life we are hurt by others—others who don't mean to hurt us, but nevertheless do. Can anyone give an example of how someone has hurt you?"

Raymond replied, "My brother. He's been shot twice and still hangs with a gang. It hurts me when he gets injured."

Ms. Soltow could see the pain on Raymond's face; tears had come to his eyes. "That's a good example of how we can be hurt by someone who doesn't mean to hurt us. I can see why that would cause pain. Does anyone else have a story to share?" she asked so as to give Raymond time to wipe his eyes. Several other students told similar stories.

Ms. Soltow redirected her attention to the rest of the class: "I'd like each of you to take out a sheet of paper and write about how someone has hurt you even though he or she didn't mean to. Be sure you state exactly how you felt at the time and how you feel about it now. I'll come around and help those who might like some assistance. Are there any questions before we start?"

The students wrote for approximately 15 minutes while Ms. Soltow circulated, encouraging them to think further about their feelings and then to express them in writing. She provided time for volunteers to share what they could about their painful experiences. Finally, she provided a list of criteria for judging the expression of ideas in the prewriting samples and allowed the remaining 15 minutes for students to evaluate their writing on the criteria distributed. She would provide a record set of criteria, including grammar, usage, and spelling on the next rewrite.

Questions for Reflection

1. Assess Ms. Soltow's strategy of having students write about how they had been hurt by someone. Was it a suitable strategy for her students, considering their backgrounds and her instructional (writing) goals? What, if anything, should she have done differently?
2. If this case was set in an economically advantaged neighborhood, would you recommend the use of Ms. Soltow's writing strategy? Why or why not?
3. What could Ms. Soltow have done to follow up with Raymond?
4. To what degree should teachers integrate students' personal feelings and personal lives outside of school into their instructional goals, in order to promote emotional literacy in their classes?
5. Briefly outline several ideas for preparing for, and responding to reports of terrorism and horriffic natural disasters in the news. List topics that you could/should address in your teaching.

Activities for Extending Thinking

1. Discuss with at least one teacher, one curriculum coordinator, and one parent those factors they believe should be considered when adapting instructional goals for students from lower socioeconomic backgrounds. Be prepared to summarize your findings in class.
2. Share appropriate aspects of your own socioeconomic history with students with whom you work. Doing so will help motivate students to do the same.
3. In addition to student needs and the nature of the subject matter, what other factors must a teacher take into account when selecting instructional goals?
4. How could you lead a P-12 class in your subject matter area in a discussion of the role of gangs in young people's lives and how they might find alternatives to gangs? What strategies could you use to discuss neglect, loneliness, and the subsequent low self-esteem and dependence that might make one more vulnerable to gang membership?
5. In the subject matter area in which you plan to teach, design a lesson plan that would address real socioemotional needs of students. Relate the lesson plan to a local, state, or national standard for teaching.

18

How Should I Grade Danielle?

A student who fails to turn in any assigned homework and contributes little to class, yet consistently gets the highest score on tests and quizzes, causes a teacher to rethink his system for assessing students.

From the first day of the fall term, Danielle, an independent Latina student, had worn black lipstick and long, often-torn shirts with names of hard-rock bands on the back, or, on warm days, the tank tops with as much exposed skin as possible. She had a six inch long tatoo on each arm. As a child of factory workers, Danielle had few friends but was usually cordial to those who approached her. She generally cooperated with her teacher, Mr. Edwards.

In class, Danielle rarely turned in a homework assignment. She worked by herself when she could; when "forced" to work in a small group, she would tend to hold back and let other group members do the talking and the work. She never volunteered to answer any questions in class discussions. When Mr. Edwards would call on her, her answer would always be correct, but short. Nevertheless, she regularly had the highest quiz and test scores. In fact, on occasion she would get a perfect score, even on the larger, more difficult comprehensive unit tests.

This combination of behaviors caused a problem for Mr. Edwards. Whereas his posted daily objectives usually required students to demonstrate understanding of concepts in homework assignments or small group discussions, his grading system was based on achievement as measured by tests. With this system, Danielle would easily earn an 'A' for the term. However, he wondered if Danielle's unwillingness to complete and turn in homework assignments and her reluctance to contribute to small groups and to class discussions should be factored into her grade. Certainly her behavior was not helpful in terms of modeling to other students the behaviors in which he would like them to engage, and the behaviors most of them needed in order to succeed.

To compound his problem, Mr. Edwards would always require self-evaluations at the end of each unit. Students were to assign to themselves some number of points out of 50, and to write a two-sentence rationale for the grade assigned. Mr. Edwards believed that, in general, it was most helpful to him to see how student self-evaluations compared with the grades he was about to assign based on the scores in his grade book. Indeed, sometimes a discrepancy between the two would help him identify an error in his record keeping, perhaps a score that inadvertently he had not recorded. For the third unit of the year, Danielle had again assigned herself a grade of 'A', using her high test scores as the basis for the grade. Mr. Edwards, a second-year teacher, often took such problems to his mentor teacher, Ms. Sundquist. Ms. Sundquist was in her ninth year as a successful teacher. "I think you need to be clear in your own mind about the outcomes you want for your students," advised Ms. Sundquist. "Your criteria and standards for assessment must be congruent with your instructional goals."

"Well," replied Mr. Edwards, "is it legitimate to have as your goals such things as 'turns in homework' and 'contributes to small and large group discussions' and the like? If these are legitimate goals, then Danielle should perhaps get a 'B' or 'C'. But when she has the highest test scores in the entire grade level, I'd have a hard time justifying that to her or her parents!"

"To be fair to students," asserted Ms. Sundquist, "the goals need to be meaningful and the students need to be clear about the criteria upon which their performances will be judged. For example, if asked to write a descriptive essay, they need to know if they will be assessed on specifics, such as organization, creativity, grammar and usage, spelling, punctuation, and/or other possible criteria for assessment. Some scholars recommend identifying levels of goal attainment on each of the standards—for example, for organization: What type of response would earn a high grade, an average grade, or a low grade? The literature in teacher education recommends that assessments be authentic; that is, that they reflect real-world applications whenever possible. I'll show you what I do if you'd like."

"Yes, I'd appreciate that," said Mr. Edwards. "I'd also like to explore strategies for using peer evaluations and portfolios, including electronic portfolios. I hear Mr. Boeck has a computer program for electronic portfolios."

"You have some challenging questions. Let's start with examples of how I design authentic performance assessments for my class. I'll bring some to our mentor–mentee meeting on Friday."

Questions for Reflection

1. What grade should Mr. Edwards assign to Danielle? What is your rationale for assigning that grade?
2. What factors influenced the grade you gave to her? Was her appearance and/or personality a factor?
3. What changes, if any, should Mr. Edwards make in his plan for assessing students? Why are those changes needed?
4. Might a student's social class and economic status affect his or her achievements? If so, in what ways?
5. What assessment techniques might be less fair and more fair to students of lower-income families? Why?
6. What strategies could you as Danielle's teacher use to address the issue of overexposure of body parts, e.g., the wearing of revealing tank tops to class?

Activities for Extending Thinking

1. Interview at least one experienced, practicing teacher to determine (a) his or her desired student outcomes for a given unit and (b) the standards and criteria for assessing those outcomes. Explore the degree to which the means of assessment are fair and supportive of students of lower-income families.
2. Interview at least one experienced practicing teacher to ascertain how, if at all, the teacher's plan for assessment and grading accommodates students of lower-income status.
3. Outline a plan to involve students in developing criteria to be used in assessing their work.

Rewarding Respectful Behavior

*A teacher uses a behavior modification plan to encourage
two students to become more respectful of classmates.*

Ms. Anderson was having trouble with two students of color in her class: Tommy, an energetic student from a low-income, blue-collar home; and Delia, a bright student from an upper-middle-class family. They often called their fellow students names—sometimes even using profanity—and did not seem to care about others' feelings. No matter how many times a day Ms. Anderson reprimanded them, they did not seem to change.

One day she offered them a deal. For every time they were thoughtful of another student—such as when they offered to help another student, when they shared, when they said nice things without name-calling or profanity—they would receive a point. When they reached 20 points, they would be allowed to choose a reward from a predetermined list that Tommy, Delia, and Ms. Anderson made together. The point total would be displayed on a chart at Ms. Anderson's desk for them to see whenever they wished.

Tommy enjoyed the challenge and began to say "please" and "thank you" to fellow students and always asked permission before using what belonged to others. He stopped making rude comments to the other students and even played with them without incident. Ms. Anderson told Tommy she was pleased with the change in his behavior.

Delia, however, continued her disrespectful ways. Ms. Anderson considered contacting Delia's parents, but a rumor that her parents were strict and harsh led her to reconsider. She decided to ask other teachers and counselors for recommendations about handling Delia's rude behavior. Perhaps her colleagues could help.

Questions for Reflection

1. To what extent have you used an incentive/reward system such as the one Ms. Anderson used with Tommy and Delia? How well did it work? Under what circumstances would you use such a system?
2. Some scholars say that low SES students are often influenced or motivated by relationships. Give two verbatim relationship-based responses to students who want to know why you (as the teacher) want them to change this behavior.
3. Identify the strengths of Ms. Anderson's system.
4. Identify the weaknesses of her system.
5. How might child-rearing practices in lower-income homes affect student behavior? Should child-rearing practices of parents or guardians affect how a teacher manages student behavior?

Activities for Extending Thinking

1. Interview parents of students of two or three different socioeconomic levels regarding the disciplinary policies and practices they prefer used at school.
2. Read a theoretical or empirical research account of the relationship between socioeconomic status and family approaches to discipline. Be prepared to share key insights with your class.
3. Design a written plan to form a student–faculty committee to write a set of rules for respect for the school. Suggest that the final draft be displayed in all classrooms, the cafeteria, and other key locations.
4. Organize with another school a student exchange program that brings together pupils of different socioeconomics backgrounds.

Design Your Own Case

Socioeconomic Status

Design a case that explores an issue of socioeconomic status in the classroom. The story can focus on a method or strategy related to a single subject matter area (e.g., English or social studies) or on a more generic method or strategy pertinent to a wider range of subject matter areas. Your issue might also relate to:

- Planning and preparation
- Classroom environment
- Instruction
- Teacher responsibilities*

In selecting a topic, reflect on recent or current field experiences, personal experiences as a student, or accounts of real classroom incidents. Include some demographic data that tell a bit about the community, school, classroom, teacher, students, and curriculum. Include at least one problem for which there is no obvious answer. Use fictitious names of persons and schools to maintain confidentiality.

Your case should be approximately two pages in length (typed, double-spaced) and should include three to four "Questions for Reflection," and one or two "Activities for Extending Thinking." Go to Resource C and use the form to design your own case.

*The four categories are from *Enhancing Professional Practice: A Framework for Teaching,* C. Danielson. 1996, Alexandria, VA: Association for Supervision and Curriculum Development.

Readings for Extending Thinking

A common bond. (2005, February). *American Teacher, 89*(5), 13.

Adams, M., Bell, L.A., and Griffin, P. (1997). *Teaching for diversity and social justice: A sourcebook.* New York: Routledge.

Archives, 10 (18). Retrieved February 14, 2003, from http://epaa.asu.edu/epaa/v10n18.

Barton, P. E. (2004). Why does the gap persist? *Educational Leadership, 62*(3), 8–13.

Carnoy, M. (1994). *Faded dreams: The politics and economics of race in America.* New York: Cambridge University Press.

Census Bureau. (1999). Statistical abstract of the United States (119th edition). Washington, DC: U.S. Government Printing Office.

Cohen, E. G. (2000). Equitable classrooms in a changing society. In M. T. Hallinan (Ed.), *Handbook of the sociology of education* (pp. 265–283). New York: Kluwer Academic/Plenum.

Darling-Hammond, L. (2001). Inequality and access to knowledge. In J. A. Banks & C. A. M. Banks (Eds.), *Handbook of research on multicultural education* (pp. 465–483). San Francisco: Jossey-Bass.

Davis, P. (1995). *If you came this way: A journey through the lives of the underclass.* New York: Wiley.

Eron, L. D., Gentry, J. H., & Schlegel, P. (Eds.). (1994). *Reason to hope: A psychosocial perspective on violence and youth.* Washington, DC: American Psychological Association.

Gans, H. (1995). *The war against the poor: The underclass and antipoverty policy.* New York: Basic.

Hochschild, J. (1995). *Facing up to the American dream: Race, class and the soul of the nation.* Princeton, NJ: Princeton University Press.

Jencks, C., & Peterson, P. E. (Eds.). (1991). *The urban underclass.* Washington, DC: Brookings Institute.

Kotlowitz, A. (1991). *There are no children here: The story of two boys growing up in the other America.* New York: Doubleday.

Kozol, J. (1991). *Savage inequalities: Children in America's schools.* New York: Crown.

Marable, M. (1995). *Beyond Black and White: Rethinking race in American politics and society.* New York: Verso.

Oliver, M., & Shapiro, T. (1995). *Black wealth/White wealth: A new perspective on racial inequality.* New York: Routledge.

Payne, R. K. (2003). No child left behind: What's really behind it all? *Part I, Instructional Leader, 16*(2), 1–3.

Payne, R. K. (1995). *A framework: Understanding and working with students and adults from poverty.* Baytown, Texas: RFT.

Rank, M. R. (2004). One nation underprivileged: Why American poverty affects us all. New York, New York: Oxford University Press.

Reay, D. (2002). Shaun's story: Troubling discourses of White working-class masculinities. *Gender and Education, 14*, 221–234.

Rose, S. J. (2000). *Social Stratification in the United States.* New York: New Press.

Timmer, D. A., Eitzen, D. S., & Talley, K. D. (1994). *Paths to homelessness: Extreme poverty and the urban housing crisis.* Boulder: Westview.

Internet Sites for Extending Thinking

http://www.ed.gov/offices/OUS/PES/esed/poverty3.html
Academic challenge for the children of poverty report analysis and highlights.

http://www.ed.gov/pubs/urbanhope/
Hope for urban education: A study of nine high-performing, high-poverty urban
   elementary schools, 1999.

http://dmoz.org/society/issues/poverty/
Contains articles & links on hunger, homelessness, & welfare as well as humanitarian
   organizations serving individuals, institutions and society, nationally and
   internationally.

http://www.src.uchicago.edu/social class/links.html
A University of Chicago list of links to web sites related to socioeconomic status. Also
   contains a helpful index of online articles on social class status.

Chapter 6

Religion

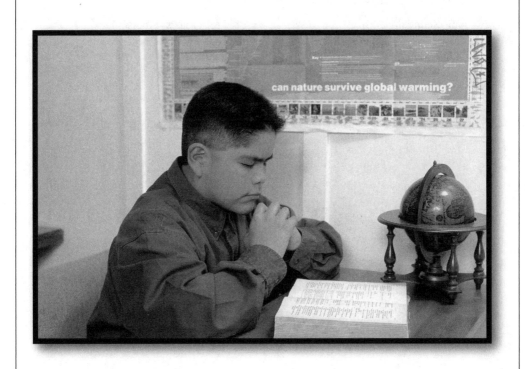

Introduction

For millions of people in this country and around the world, religion or spirituality is a significant part of their lives. Even adults who do not believe in a religion, usually admit that religions have long been an important part of the history of the world. Many students, including many immigrant children, have seen their people, even relatives, willing to die for deeply held religious values. To many, religion has been, is, and always will be, a vitally important force in the world.

At the same time, there are those who believe that religion should be relegated to the home and church, synagogue, mosque, or other place of worship. "Separation of church and state" is a phrase that deters many teachers from the slightest mention of religion in the classroom.

The cases in Chapter 6, "Religion," invite inquiry into issues that have ramifications for curriculum content, teaching methods (e.g., teaching about values), scheduling of curricular and extracurricular activities, and classroom and school policies and rules (e.g., dress codes involving religious wear and religious activities). Terms and concepts that often arise in the discussion of these cases include:

anti-Semitism	religious symbols
Islam	separation of school and state
Judaism	spirituality
provisions of the First Amendment to the Constitution	values

Definitions of key terms are located in the glossary of this text.

Isn't the Christmas Tree a Christian Symbol?

A classroom Christmas tree and other winter holiday symbols cause students to question the teacher's intent.

It was the first week of December. The previous day Ms. Halverson had added to her bulletin boards some holiday wishes, including "Merry Christmas," "Happy Hanukkah," and "Happy Kwanza." In addition, she had placed a two-foot-tall Christmas tree in the front corner of the room by her desk.

Several of her students had entered the room a few minutes before class was to begin. The students were of Russian, Chinese, and Egyptian heritage. They made a few comments to one another and then addressed Ms. Halverson: "Ms. Halverson, you told us to let you know if we felt that our classroom was not as inclusive as it could possibly be. Well, isn't the Christmas tree a symbol of the Christian religion?" asked Yen. "And by having a Christmas tree, aren't you emphasizing one religion over another?"

Ms. Halverson nodded as Yen spoke: "Actually, it's a pre-Christian symbol that arose in Europe. But I only meant to acknowledge it as one of the most prevalent historical and cultural symbols in the United States."

Yen responded, "So you didn't mean to promote Christianity?"

"No," replied Ms. Halverson. "But I'm glad that you raised the issue. I now realize that I need to clarify for the class just what my intentions are regarding the tree. Thanks for being sensitive to those who might have other interpretations. It's exactly this kind of feedback that I need to make our class more inclusive! Perhaps you and the class can offer some other suggestions for making our room look more inclusive during the holidays." The students seemed eager to help.

Questions for Reflection

1. Should Ms. Halverson have placed a Christmas tree in her room? Why or why not?
2. How adequate was Ms. Halverson's explanation of her intent to the students? What, if anything, would make it more adequate?
3. What factors should affect a teacher's decision to display religious symbols?

4. Comment on the relationship between the teacher and Yen. What did Ms. Halverson say or do that would tend to affect her relationship with him?

5. What could Ms. Halverson and her class do to extend their new knowledge beyond their own classroom, i.e., to affect school policy?

Activities for Extending Thinking

1. Discuss with a school administrator the policies in his/her school regarding the use or display of objects that have or could have some religious meaning. Summarize your key insights in writing.

2. List school practices with regard to religion that are allowed by law. List practices not allowed by law. Summarize your findings in writing.

3. Examine the musical selections of school orchestra, band, and choir to determine the degree of cultural diversity represented. Share your findings (in a supportive/constructive way) with teachers involved with those programs.

Case 21

My Persuasive Essay Is "Why We Should Follow Jesus"

To foster a feeling of ownership in their persuasive essays,
a teacher allows students the opportunity to choose
the topic they will present to the class.

Mr. Kauls had taught middle school English for 10 years. One of his favorite units was persuasive writing. Although students were typically reluctant when it came to talking to the class, they seemed to become very motivated—even excited—to talk about something in which they truly believed. Each year in a letter to parents, Mr. Kauls made it clear that his goal was to actively involve students in the process of writing and speaking persuasively, not to condone the specific topic chosen. How could he? Last year students spoke on "Why Abortion Should Be Available to All," "Eliminating Affirmative Action," "Why Schools Should Put Pop Machines in Each Room," and "Evidence That the White Race Is Superior," and he certainly did not agree with the premise in all of those reports.

Of course, Mr. Kauls did his best at structuring the project for students' success. Before they presented, he modeled for the class the presentation of a piece of persuasive writing of two students from a previous year, as well as one of his own. Students could clearly see how it should be done.

In addition, Mr. Kauls collected and made written suggestions on the prewriting phase of each student's persuasive essay. After rewriting, he again collected and graded the second draft. By the time it was their turn to present orally to the class, students knew that Mr. Kauls supported their plan.

Finally, Mr. Kauls made it very clear that classmates must show the presenter the utmost respect. Consequences of showing even a hint of disrespect included detention and a phone call to their parents.

As in previous years, when Mr. Kauls first explained the assignment to the class, he had students write down the topics about which they would like to write and speak. Michael, a capable student respected by classmates for his academic and athletic abilities, as well as for his personal qualities, listed "Why We Should Follow Jesus" as the topic of his persuasive writing and speaking project.

When it was Michael's turn to present, he began by acknowledging that he knew it was risky to write and speak about his selected topic, but that he believed it was so much more important than his alternative, "Why We Should All Visit Alaska." After introductory comments, he outlined his arguments: "First, following Jesus provides a reason for living, a purpose for life, that of caring for others. Second, following Jesus assures us of eternal life, and offers salvation. Third, following Jesus helps us cope with our daily lives. I don't know how persons handle stress without the comfort that comes through prayer." Michael continued, "Because we cannot understand all the mysteries of God, we do at times need a strong faith. Finally, Jesus is a great gift. While there have been many kings throughout history, Jesus is the only one who died for us." Michael cited what he considered evidence that Jesus had divine power. He paused for a moment, then took his seat. The class applause for his presentation was louder than it had been for the other reports.

Mr. Kauls commented that Michael's report had been well organized and clearly presented and that he had more than satisfied the criteria for a good persuasive essay.

After class Greg and Dion, two students whom Michael knew only slightly, approached Michael with smiles: "I didn't know you were a Christian. We are, too. You did a good job on your report."

"Thanks," replied Michael. "Where do you guys go to church?" They talked as they walked to their lockers. "See you tomorrow," they said as each headed off to a different classroom.

The next morning Mr. Kauls checked his phone messages. One was from Mr. Warren, the father of Billy Warren, one of his students. Mr. Kauls knew that the Warrens were of the Mormon faith. The other message was from Sylvia Bernstein, mother of James. The Bernsteins were Jewish. Mr. Kauls wondered if it was a coincidence that two parents who had never contacted him before were requesting an audience the day after Michael's presentation.

After school that day Mr. Kauls' suspicions were realized. When he returned their calls, both parents questioned the propriety of allowing a student to do a persuasive essay on a religious topic. "I thought that schools were prohibited from evangelism," commented Mr. Warren.

Mr. Kauls reminded them of the letter that he had sent prior to the beginning of the new unit. His conversations with both parents seemed to quell their concerns. Yet, he could not help but wonder what else he might have done to make the persuasive essay activity more satisfactory to both students and parents.

Questions for Reflection

1. What else, if anything, would you have done to prevent or address parental concerns about presenting a persuasive essay on religion in the public school classroom?
2. What limits, if any, would you have set on student choice of topic?
3. Construct a verbatim response to the Warrens and the Bernsteins regarding their concerns.
4. The First Amendment provides for the inclusion of certain religious references in the public schools. For example, it provides for books such as the Bible (Christianity), Tanakh (Judaism), Qur'an (Islam), or Tripitaka (Buddhism) to be used as historical or literary resources. In what other ways can religion be included in the public school classroom?
5. Identify several lesson plans in your own subject matter area that would draw on religious references.

Activities for Extending Thinking

1. Discuss the issue in this case with a practicing teacher. Elicit ideas for preventing, guiding, and responding to the series of events in the story. Inquire about similar experiences that the teacher may have had. Summarize key insights in writing.
2. Select one of the "Readings for Extending Thinking" at the end of this section. Outline its key claims or assertions in writing, and give a personal reaction to each.
3. Discuss with parents or teachers in your community the issue of diversity within a religion, (e.g., Christianity). List areas of potential conflict for students due to such diversity. Give concrete examples of problems and ways they could be addressed in your classroom.
4. List on one page what the constitution allows and prohibits with respect to integrating religion into the classroom?

Case 22

Planning for Religious Diversity: Special Needs of Muslim Students

In light of increasing numbers of Islamic children in the nation's schools, a local teacher examines the background and special religion-based needs of her Islamic students.

Ms. Bush worked hard to be sensitive to the needs of students of diverse backgrounds. She had become aware that the fastest growing group of students in her school was that of the Muslim faith. She had seen data suggesting that Islam has become the second-largest religion in the United States. She also knew that over one billion people–one-fifth of the world's population–were Muslim, that about 14 percent of all immigrants entering the United States are Muslim, and that while one-third of Muslims living in the United States are African-American, several million Americans from various ethnic backgrounds have adopted the religion of Islam within the last quarter century. She was curious about the special needs and interests that the students in her classroom might have.

Ms. Bush requested and received material from her local Islamic Education Foundation Center. She read from a brochure entitled "You've Got a Muslim Child in Your Room: The Needs of Muslim Children in the Public School" (Islamic Education Foundation, 2000):

> Muslim students have the following needs and requirements: Muslim students, from the onset of puberty, may not sit in close proximity to students of the opposite sex, and they may not interact closely with them. Thus, girls and boys should be assigned to sit near others of their own sex, and should not be assigned to group or partner activities with members of the opposite sex.

Because she was familiar with research on best teaching practice, Ms. Bush had always intentionally created heterogeneous groups with respect to gender, race, learning style, and other factors. She wondered if her students would want to follow the guidelines stated in the brochure strictly, and if they did, how she would accommodate them.

As she read further in the brochure, she learned that Muslim students who follow their religious tenets strictly may not participate in plays, social parties, proms, dating, or other such activities that involve close interaction with the opposite sex. In addition, they may not participate in any event or activity related to Halloween, Christmas, Valentine's Day, or Easter because such events have social and religious connotations contrary to the Islamic faith. In addition, they may not pay allegiance to the flag, and they should not be asked to stand and sing the national anthem or the national anthem of any country even that of their homeland.

The brochure stated also that while well-meaning educators have expressed concern for Muslim students who are "deprived" of participating in activities of their non-Muslim peers, Muslim parents love their children. Therefore, teachers should refrain from expressing well-intended but inappropriate "sympathy" or disapproval of parental requests. Ms. Bush decided that she would refer additional guidelines related to physical education and prayer in the schools to her colleagues who would be most directly affected.

Ms. Bush wondered how she should react to the information she had just read. How should the special needs of her Muslim students affect her planning for the coming fall?

Questions for Reflection

1. If you were Ms. Bush, what questions might you want to ask your Muslim students and/or their parents about the special religious needs stated in the brochure?
2. Assume that certain parents of Muslim students are quite concerned about following the tenets/principles of their faith, and that their child is moderately concerned. How, if at all, would you accommodate the need of that student to be grouped only with persons of the same sex?
3. Would you arrange meaningful alternate activities for students of the Islamic faith who could not participate in holidays such as Christmas, Halloween, and so on? If so, what types of activities might you offer?
4. How would you respond if a Muslim parent asked that his or her child not be required to say the pledge of allegiance to the flag and/or sing the U.S. national anthem? State your response verbatim.
5. Identify other religious groups and the special needs that students of each faith might have. How might you alter your curriculum or instruction to accommodate those needs?
6. How could you as a teacher prevent or respond to 9-11 anti–Middle-Eastern sentiment in your classroom resulting from terrorist acts or threats?

Activities for Extending Thinking

1. Obtain from community agencies and religious organizations information about the religious needs of students in your school. If your school does not have students from a variety of religious backgrounds, obtain information about religions with which your students will likely interact in their lives beyond P–12 schooling. In general, what types of things should students know in order to interact with others of differing religions?
2. Interview students about how schools and teachers can become more aware of special religious needs of students from diverse religious backgrounds. List practical strategies that teachers can use to accommodate students with special religious needs.

3. Interview school officials in your area about current policies and practices that relate to religious affiliation. Ask about religious issues that tend to arise more frequently (e.g., find out how the school or district conducts winter holiday celebrations [traditionally called "Christmas Programs"]). Do they read scripture, sing religious songs, display traditional and/or nontraditional scenes, etc.? Ask how the school has addressed such issues.

4. How could you integrate information about religious diversity into the discipline(s) you will teach? List specific topics that you might include in certain units you are likely to teach.

Design Your Own Case

Religion

Design a case that would help classmates explore issues related to religious diversity. The story can focus on a method or strategy related to a single subject matter area (e.g., English or social studies) or on a more generic method or strategy pertinent to a wider range of subject matter areas. Your issue might also relate to:

- Planning and preparation
- Classroom environment
- Instruction
- Teacher responsibilities*

In selecting a topic, reflect on recent or current field experiences, personal experiences as a student, or accounts of real classroom incidents. Include some demographic data that tell a bit about the community, school, classroom, teacher, students, and curriculum. Include at least one problem for which there is no obvious answer. Use fictitious names of persons and schools to maintain confidentiality. Your case should be approximately two pages in length (typed, double-spaced) and should include three to four "Questions for Reflection," and one or two "Activities for Extending Thinking." Go to Resource C and use the form to design your own case.

*The four categories are from *Enhancing Professional Practice: A Framework for Teaching*, by C. Davidson, 1996. Alexandria, VA: Association for Supervision and Curriculum Development.

Readings for Extending Thinking

Al-Ani, S. H. (1995). Muslims in America and Arab Americans. In C. L. Bennett (Ed.), *Comprehensive multicultural education: Theory and practice* (3rd ed., p. 139). Boston: Allyn & Bacon.

Black, S. (2003, April). Teaching about religion. *The American School Board Journal, 190*(4), 50.

Crim, K., Bullard, R., & Shinn, L. D. (Eds.). (1981). *The perennial dictionary of world religions*. San Francisco: HarperCollins.

Doerr, E. (2005, March). Much to learn from Newfoundland. *Phi Delta Kappan, 86*(7), 559.

Feingold, H. L. (1995). *Bearing witness: How America and its Jews responded to the Holocaust*. Syracuse, NY: Syracuse University Press.

First Amendment to the Constitution of the United States, 1791.

Freitas, D., & Rotherham, A. (2004, January 7). Teaching about religion. *Education Week, 23*(16), 37.

Haltom, B. (2000). I'll keep praying for my football team. *Tennessee Bar Journal, 36*(8), 34–35.

Holliday, L. (1995). *Children in the Holocaust and WWII: Their secret diaries*. New York: Pocket Books.

Islamic Education Foundation. (2000). *You've got a Muslim child in your room: The needs of Muslim children in the public school*. Minneapolis, MN: Islamic Education Foundation.

Kirmani, M. H., & Laster, B. P. (1999). Responding to religious diversity in classrooms. *Educational Leadership, 56*(7), 61–63.

Lustig, A. (1995). *Children of the Holocaust*. Evanston, IL: Northwestern University Press.

Markowitz, R. J. (1993). *My daughter, the teacher: Jewish teachers in the New York City schools*. New Brunswick, NJ: Rutgers University Press.

Marks, J. (1993). *The hidden children: Secret survivors of the Holocaust*. New York: Ballantine.

Marshall, J. M. (2004, January). How teachers can still teach about religion. *The Education Digest, 69*(5), 23–27.

Marty, W. R. (1998). Christians in the academy: Overcoming the silence. *Journal of Interdisciplinary Studies, 10*(1–2), 1–16.

Not the Last Word. (2000). *America, 183*(2), 3.

Ooka Pang, V., & Barba, R. H. (1995). The power of culture: Building culturally affirming instruction. In C. A. Grant (Ed.), *Educating for diversity: An anthology of multicultural voices* (pp. 345–356). Boston: Allyn & Bacon.

Rabinove, S. (2000). The 10 Commandments and public schools: Shall we post the penalties too? *Church & State, 53*(10), 21.

Scherer, M. M. (1998). Linking education with the spiritual. *Educational Leadership, 56*(4), 5.

Smith, J. Z., & Green, W. S. (Eds.). (1995). *The HarperCollins dictionary of religion.* San Francisco: HarperCollins.

Uphoff, J. K. (1993). Religious diversity and education. In J. A. Banks & C. A. McGee Banks (Eds.), *Multicultural education: Issues and perspectives* (2nd ed., p. 46). Boston: Allyn & Bacon.

Werner, H. (1992). *Fighting back: A memoir of Jewish resistance in WW II.* New York: Columbia University Press.

Wiesel, E. (1986). *Night* (25th anniv. ed.). New York: Bantam.

Internet Sites for Extending Thinking

http://www.nmajh.org
Virtual tours of online exhibitions, comparative timeline that tracks U.S. history, U.S. Jewish history, and world Jewish history.

http://www.clsnet.org
Christian Legal Society Web site on religious expression in public schools.

http://www.nsba.org
National School Board Web site on religious expression in schools.

http://www.academicinfo.net/religindex.html
Libraries, directories, and other resources on a wide variety of religions.

http://www.academicinfo.net/Religiontolerance.html
References on religious tolerance/freedom.

http://www.looksmart.com
Click on "Religion & Belief," click on "Islam," click on "Education," and finally click on "Online Courses."

http://www.edweek.org/tm/vol-07/06relig.h07
An excellent article that includes an overview of the issue and highlights the author's visits to classrooms where teaching about religion is incorporated into the curriculum.

http://www.cie.org
The Council on Islamic Education's mission is to support public education, with lessons, teaching units, and other resources for educators.

http://www.teachingaboutreligion.org
This site provides academic information and materials for educators, especially on teaching about religion in social studies and religious studies.

http://www.adl.org/adl.asp
The Anti-Defamation League provides materials on anti-Semitism, civil rights, extremism, the Holocaust, Israel, interfaith, and curriculum development.

Chapter 7

Special Needs

Introduction

In this text, the area of special needs or exceptionality includes students who are identified as gifted or talented as well as students with disabilities. Disability in its broadest sense includes: perceptual challenges, e.g., visual and hearing, as well as learning disabilities; illness-related, e.g., multiple sclerosis, AIDS; physical, e.g., cerebral palsy; developmental, e.g., Down syndrome; psychiatric, e.g., chronic depression, bipolar; mobility, e.g., quadriplegia, paraplegia; and environmental, e.g., asthma and sensitivities to allergies (Adams, et al., 1997).

Discrimination against students with disabilities (also called "ableism") takes many forms in schools, including the use of the terms "retard" or "retarded" as a pejorative, teasing or bullying, telling jokes about persons with disabilities, and excluding exceptional students from groups, activities, and events.

Special needs or exceptional students are those who require attention from teachers and schools that is beyond that and/or different from attention needed by students without special challenges. As in the case of other oppressed groups, special needs students often come to feel that others view them as less worthy. Such perceptions often lead to feelings of low self-worth, resulting in reduced interest in school academic and social endeavors.

Discussion of cases in Chapter 7 often results in the use of the following terms and concepts:

ableism	Individuals with Disabilities Education Act
accommodation	(IDEA)
culturally and linguistically diverse (CLD)	Individuals with Disabilities Education
disability	Improvement Act (IDEIA)
grouping strategies	learning disabled
Individualized Education Program (IEP)	

Definitions of key terms are included in the glossary of this text.

23

We Only Meant It as a Joke

*Several students "play a joke" on a female classmate by telling
a learning-disabled pupil that she has a crush on him.*

Mr. Carr consistently demonstrated respect for all his students. All students, including special-needs students, had a chance to work in heterogeneous, cooperative groups, share leadership roles, and generally contribute equally to classroom life. Mr. Carr was careful to praise and encourage all students equally.

One of the classroom procedures posted on the front wall was "Respect others." Students understood what this meant—they had been given numerous specific concrete examples on the first day of class.

For the first six weeks of the term, Mr. Carr's students honored the procedures listed. Then one day, several students were moved to have what they considered fun with Mia, one of their classmates. They suggested to Mike, a learning-disabled student, that Mia had expressed an interest in him and that he should call her and ask her to be his girlfriend. They intended that the "joke" would be on Mia. That evening Mike called Mia. Mia politely replied that she did not want a boyfriend.

When Mr. Carr heard what had happened, he immediately thought about how he would enforce the classroom rule that students respect others. Of course, the perpetrators would have to pay the consequences established on the first day of school. Mr. Carr believed in being consistent in maintaining standards for behavioral conduct. Now he was faced with the question of how to best make this situation a learning experience.

Questions for Reflection

1. Is it possible for a teacher to establish, ahead of time, rules and consequences for an offense such as the one in this case? If so, how?
2. What consequence(s) would be appropriate for the students who created the problem for Mike and Mia?
3. What might you say to Mike that would be helpful to him? What would be some responses that you would not want to make?
4. What would you say to Mia? What would be some responses you would not want to make?
5. What could Mr. Carr do to help all of his students be more respectful of those with special needs?
6. Should the teacher's response have been different if this had transpired between regular education students? If so, in what way?

Activities for Extending Thinking

1. Discuss with at least one special-education teacher the types of conflicts that most often occur between students with special needs and (a) teachers and (b) regular education students. What can teachers do to prevent such problems?

2. Discuss with a special-needs student what he or she would like general education teachers to do to improve interaction between special-needs students and (a) non–special-needs students and (b) teachers. Summarize your findings in writing and be prepared to share in class.

3. In consultation with teachers and administration, design an orientation program that addresses the needs of students with mental, physical, or sensory challenges. If such a program already exists, in consultation with special-needs students, assess its adequacy and suggest improvements.

Case 24

Structuring for Success in a Mainstreamed Classroom

By employing a number of special instructional strategies, a teacher tries to ensure that students with learning disabilities will succeed.

Mr. French believed that mainstreaming students with mental and physical disabilities would benefit not only those with the disability but the nondisabled as well. Over the past four years, he had given much thought to how best to arrange his instruction to ensure that both groups of students would learn. With the disabled students, for example, he regularly limited problems so that they focused their learning on a single concept, included in assignments only material that was essential to the task at hand, and collected student work as soon as it was completed so that he could give immediate feedback. In addition, he held frequent, short, one-on-one conferences in which he asked each student to restate his or her responsibilities with respect to the assignment. Finally, he had a corner of his room set aside for mainstreamed students so that they could choose to work in a quiet, uncrowded area, and they frequently took advantage of the opportunity he provided.

On the third day of school, Mr. French was planning his lesson for the next day. His goal was to have students learn a number of social skills that they could use in his class, as well as in others. He would begin with listening skills and skills for asking questions, for these were two skill groups with which learning disabled (LD), attention deficit/hyperactive disorder (ADHD), and other disabled and nondisabled students often had trouble. He would have students work in groups of five. There were five learning-disabled students in his class this term, and he would have them form one group. Mr. French reasoned that having them work together would give each student a feeling of support, knowing that each had a learning disability and no one would make fun of them. Once the groups were formed, he would briefly define and model for them one of the four good listening skills: paraphrasing, empathizing, asking open questions, and asking clarifying questions, and then he would allow them to practice each skill through role play. If he modeled one skill at a time, students would be able to focus on that skill and not be confused with too many new concepts at once. After the groups were finished practicing the skills, the class as a large group would discuss the effects of the role play—for example, whether it was easier or harder to use the skills than they had expected and what problems they had experienced.

Each previous year, the students had seemed to enjoy the role-play activity. Mr. French always believed that students had achieved their goals in the activity.

Questions for Reflection

1. Which of the learning activities used by Mr. French would you support as being consistent with his goal of maximizing learning for both the disabled and nondisabled students? Why? Which would you oppose? Why?
2. Was Mr. French's grouping strategy appropriate for both disabled and nondisabled students? Give evidence from research to support your answer.
3. How can teachers organize the physical space in the classroom to facilitate learning for a diverse student population? Consider factors such as arrangement of furniture, use of teaching aids (e.g., overheads, flip charts, and computer presentation programs), and student accessibility to learning resources.

Activities for Extending Thinking

1. Discuss with at least two special-education teachers pedagogical techniques appropriate for students with various types of special needs. List grouping strategies, common sources of student error, and proven subject-based pedagogy for each kind of special need. In addition to identifying patterns of learning for each group, identify individual differences within those patterns. Provide demographic data on the number of students in special education in their school, including the number of males, females, students of color, and bilingual students, as well as the number mainstreamed.
2. Using written resources or special-education teachers, identify strategies for assessing and grading special-needs students. Summarize your findings in two to three pages.
3. Identify steps that teachers and other school personnel could take to advocate for students whose parents refuse to have them tested and/or admitted into a special-needs program.

Case 25

Anthony, Please Don't Push: Designing an IEP

A special-education teacher offers help in diagnosing classroom behavior of a student with special needs and in designing an appropriate Individualized Education Program (IEP) for him and for others.

Ms. Melby was an experienced special-education teacher. She loved working with special-needs students and was an ardent advocate for them. She believed in working closely with regular-education teachers who had mainstreamed students in their classrooms.

During her third-hour preparation period, Ms. Shilala, a fourth-year teacher, entered Ms. Melby's room. "Got a minute?" she asked.

Ms. Melby replied, "Yes, of course. Come in."

Ms. Shilala proceeded. "I'd like to ask you about Anthony Martinez. I believe he is in your special-ed class, is he not?"

"Yes—he's a hard worker," replied Ms. Melby.

"He's generally cooperative and pretty thorough in his work for me, too," agreed Ms. Shilala. "But one thing I don't understand is that he has a bad habit of pushing his class-mates. It doesn't matter who it is. In fact, he pushes those he considers to be his friends more than anyone else. He'll be getting along fine with them and then, all of a sudden, he pushes."

"Yes," said Ms. Melby, "I think I know why. Anthony recently has been diagnosed with a vision problem. He can't see things close to him. He pushes things away, even people, so that he can see them more clearly. I've been working with him on that. You might want to explain the situation to your students. I'd also recommend that you remind him not to push, but also to ask others to step back."

"That explains it!" sighed Ms. Shilala. "I knew he wasn't a malicious kid! Thank you." After a moment, she asked, "While I'm here, may I ask one more question?"

"Sure," said Ms. Melby with a smile.

"I'm meeting tomorrow with a team to design an Individualized Education Program [IEP] for Anthony. I expect his parents, social worker, doctor, the school nurse, and Ms. Hanson, our new special-ed teacher, to attend. What are the key issues to build into the plan from a teacher's point of view?"

"Well," said Ms. Melby, "I like to consider individual style. Is the student a visual learner and perhaps one who sees the big picture; that is, a global learner? Is he or she one who learns best from manipulating concrete objects, or are abstract ideas preferred? I also think the Howard Gardner concept of multiple intelligences is important—that is, does a given pupil seem to be more able to handle ideas analytically or logically? Is he or she pretty adept interpersonally or intrapersonally? How about kinesthetic or other abilities?"

"That's a lot to think about, especially when I have six students who need IEPs!" said Ms. Shilala in a worried tone. "I don't know if I can handle six different plans that require that much detail!"

"I'd be happy to help you," said Ms. Melby. "I know quite a bit about each of them already."

"Oh, great. I'd appreciate that," sighed Ms. Shilala.

Questions for Reflection

1. What is the "moral of the story" about Anthony? In other words, what general principle(s) should we develop to help us deal with apparent misbehavior in a classroom?
2. Does Ms. Melby's advice regarding how to handle Anthony seem appropriate? What, if anything, would you change?
3. Assess Ms. Melby's response regarding the development of IEPs. What, if anything, would you change?
4. What other issues regarding the behavior of students with special needs are of concern to you?
5. Positive relationships with colleagues can benefit students as well as teachers. How can you foster faculty and staff collegial relationships that would benefit students with special needs?
6. What can schools do to provide more effective programs and services for pupils with special needs?

Activities for Extending Thinking

1. Talk with a student or two identified as having special needs. Consider students with physical and mental challenges as well as those with inherited or acquired crack cocaine addictions or AIDS. Discuss the needs being met by the school as well as those that could be better met.
2. Discuss with school officials methods of diagnosing special-needs students. Inquire about the assessment instruments used and the persons who make the decisions about classifying students as culturally and linguistically diverse (CLD). Summarize your findings in writing. Include a comment on the degree to which the evaluators are sensitive to minority and majority students, and the degree to which the evaluators are willing to assume an advocacy role for CLD students.
3. Interview a special-education teacher about specific methods regular education teachers in your subject matter area might use to meet the special needs of students.

Case | 26

Inaccessibility of Web Sites to Students Who Are Blind

A student who is blind finds it impossible to access Web sites designed to take advantage of the graphic capabilities of browsers.

Amanda was a bright, creative, and cooperative student. Blind from birth, she had faced and overcome the many physical, intellectual, and social challenges she encountered. Usually optimistic, she could, like sighted students, have days when she felt like a victim of circumstance. Today was one of those days. Mr. Grant, Amanda's social studies teacher, had taken the class to the computer lab to give them the opportunity to locate Internet resources for their assigned projects. When Amanda raised her hand for help, Mr. Grant responded.

"Yes, Amanda? May I help you?" he asked.

"I'm having trouble with some of the Web sites. The ones with text are accessible—my computer can read the responses aloud. However, those with graphical Web browsers are inaccessible—my computer can't report pictures. I get lost!" she said with frustration in her voice.

"I understand," replied Mr. Grant. "Tai is working on a related topic, and in fact, she has collected nearly all the citations that she will need for her project. I'll ask her to help you, if that's okay with you."

"That's cool," said Amanda. "We get along well, and I'm sure it won't take long. I already have several text-based sites that I can use."

"You may want to start with the Web page 'Bobby.' As you know, it will display the page and highlight the features that would be difficult or impossible for a person who is visually disabled to use," added Mr. Grant.

"I will. I've used it before. Thanks for your help," said Amanda appreciatively.

Tai accepted Mr. Grant's request that she help Amanda. She was proud to have been selected to play the role of teacher.

Questions for Reflection

1. Assess Mr. Grant's response to Amanda's problem. How, if at all, would you change it?
2. What other technological challenges exist for students with special needs? (For example, in the future, people who are deaf may have trouble using full-motion video transmission over the Internet unless text captions are included on the screen along with the images.)

3. Design a social-action activity through which your students attempt to rectify a technology-based injustice toward students with special needs. (For example, communicate with the World Wide Web Consortium [www.w3.org] in Cambridge, England, or directly with designers to ensure that standards are in place to protect persons with special needs.)

Activities for Extending Thinking

1. Select a resource from the "Readings for Extending Thinking" list at the end of this section or from another source, such as your primary text. Summarize key insights related to the use of technology with special-needs students.
2. Interview a special-education resource teacher or a computer resource teacher regarding programs he or she would recommend for the special-needs students you teach (or will teach). List at least three recommended programs and cite their strengths, weaknesses, and how they relate to general course goals.
3. Interview a teacher in your licensure area about ways in which, using computers, he or she accommodates students at varying levels of knowledge and skill. List several guidelines that you could recommend to your classmates. Summarize your findings in writing (one to two pages).

Design Your Own Case

Special Needs

Design a case that would help classmates explore issues related to exceptionality in schools. The story can focus on a method or strategy related to a single subject matter area (e.g., English or social studies) or on a more generic method or strategy pertinent to a wider range of subject matter areas. Your issue might also relate to:

- Planning and preparation
- Classroom environment
- Instruction
- Teacher responsibilities*

In selecting a topic, reflect on recent or current field experiences, personal experiences as a student, or accounts of real classroom incidents. Include some demographic data that tell a bit about the community, school, classroom, teacher, students, and curriculum. Include at least one problem for which there is no obvious solution. Use fictitious names of persons and schools to maintain confidentiality. Your case should be approximately two pages in length (typed, double-spaced) and should include three to four "Questions for Reflection," and one or two "Activities for Extending Thinking." Go to Resource C and use the form to design your own case.

*The four categories are from *Enhancing Professional Practice: A Framework for Teaching,* by C. Danielson, 1996, Alexandria, VA: Association for Supervision and Curriculum Development.

Readings for Extending Thinking

Adams, M., Bell, L. A., and Griffin, P. (1997). *Teaching for diversity and social justice: A sourcebook.* New York: Routledge.

Artiles, A. J., & Tvent, S. C. (1994). Overrepresentation of minority students in special education: A continuing debate. *Journal of Special Education, 27,* 410–437.

Carrasquillo, A. L., & Rodriguez, V. (1995). *Language minority students in the mainstream classroom.* Bristol, PA: Taylor & Francis.

Correa, V. I., & Heward, W. L. (2000). Special education in a culturally diverse society. In W. L. Heward, *Exceptional children: An introduction to special education* (6th ed., pp. 82–114). Upper Saddle River, NJ: Merrill/Prentice Hall.

Ford, D. Y. (1998). The underrepresentation of minority students in gifted education: Problems and promises in recruitment and retention. *Journal of Special Education, 32,* 4–14.

Fuchs, D., & Fuchs, L. S. (1995). Sometimes separate is better. *Educational Leadership, 52* (4), 22–25.

Fuchs, D., & Fuchs, L. S. (2003). Inclusion versus full inclusion. In W. L. Heward, *Exceptional children: An introduction to special education* (7th ed., pp. 80–81). Upper Saddle River, NJ: Merrill/Prentice Hall.

Giangreco, M. F. (2003). Moving toward inclusion. In W. L. Heward, *Exceptional children: An introduction to special education* (7th ed., pp. 78–79). Upper Saddle River, NJ: Merrill/Prentice Hall.

Giangreco, M. F., Cloniger, C. J., & Iverson, V. S. (1998). *Choosing options and accommodations for children: A guide to educational planning for students with disabilities* (2nd ed.). Baltimore: Paul H. Brookes.

Gottlieb, J., & Atter, M. (1995). *Overrepresentation of children of color referred to special education.* New York: New York University Department of Teaching and Learning.

Heward, W. L. (1996). *Exceptional children: An introduction to special education* (5th ed.). Upper Saddle River, NJ: Merrill/Prentice Hall.

Hill, J. L. (1999). *Meeting the needs of students with special physical and health care needs.* Upper Saddle River, NJ: Merrill/Prentice Hall.

Individuals with Disabilities Act of 1990. (1990). P. L. No 101-476, 20 U.S.C. 1400–1485.

Janney, R. E., Snell, M. E., Beers, M. K., & Raynes, M. (1995). Integrating students with moderate and severe disabilities into general education classes. *Exceptional Children, 61*(5), 425–439.

Kauffman, J. M., & Hallahan, D. K. (1995). *The illusion of full inclusion: A comprehensive critique of a current special education bandwagon.* Austin, TX: PRO-ED.

Meyer, L. H., & Park, H. S. (1999). Contemporary most promising practices for people with disabilities. In J. S. Scotti & L. H. Meyer (Eds.), *Behavioral intervention: Principles, models, and practices* (pp. 25–45). Baltimore: Paul H. Brookes.

Ohoven, M., Stern, S., Stipe, M., Vince, W. (Producers), & Dannelly, B. (Director). (2004). *Saved!* [Motion picture]. United States: United Artists.

Oswald, D. P., Coutinho, M. J., Best, A. M., & Singh, N. N. (1999). Ethnic representation in special education: The influence of school-related economic and demographic variables. *Journal of Special Education, 32*, 194–206.

Rainforth, B., York, J., & MacDonald, C. (1992). *Collaborative teams for students with severe disabilities: Integrating therapy and educational services.* Baltimore: Paul H. Brookes.

Ryba, K., Selby, L., & Nolan, P. (1995). Computers empower students with special needs. *Educational Leadership, 53*(2), 82–87.

Sapon-Shevin, M. (1999). *Because we can change the world: A practical guide to building cooperative, inclusive classroom communities.* Boston: Allyn & Bacon.

Trent, S. C., Artiles, A. J., & Englert, C. S. (1998). From deficit thinking to social constructivism: A review of theory, research, and practice in special education. In *Review of research in education, 23*, 277–307. Washington, DC: American Educational Research Association.

Yell, M. L. (1995). Least restrictive environment, inclusion, and students with disabilities: A legal analysis. *Journal of Special Education, 28*, 389–404.

Internet Sites for Extending Thinking

http://ericec.org

Sponsored by the Educational Resources Information Center (ERIC), this site is a clearinghouse for data on the disabilities and gifted education. The site features links to Web pages containing fact sheets, digests, laws, research, and other subjects, as well as to online discussions groups, an FAQ, and databases relevant to the subject.

http://www.ldonline.org/

This site, run by the Learning Project at WETA, offers a wealth of information, via internal links to numerous data pages, on various LDs themselves, the issues surrounding LD in education, and other information. In addition, you can take part in online discussion, sign up for a free online newsletter, or submit questions about LDs.

http://seriweb.com

Billed as "Special Education Resources on the Internet," SERI is basically an extensive page of links to more links, covering almost every aspect of special education. From legal issues to definitions of various disabilities, discussion groups, organization listings—if there's a Web site covering some aspect of special education, you will doubtless find it here on one of the many secondary pages.

http://www.educationworld.com/special ed/

Education World brings you this megasite, which contains a vast assortment of special education information that is both wide and deep: articles (including an archive), reviews, resource listings, databases, reference centers, and more. The site is a breeze to navigate and easy to read.

http://www.cec.sped.org/index.html

Council for Exceptional Children site includes publications and products, professional standards, discussion forums, a link to ERIC Clearinghouse on disabilities and gifted education, career connections, and professional development training events, all on topics relating to exceptionality.

http://hoagiesgifted.org

Click on "educators" for information on books, programs, curriculum, and theories on gifted education.

Chapter 8

Sexual Orientation

Introduction

Some, including this writer, prefer the term "affectional orientation," because it places emphasis on aspects of the self beyond the sexual aspect, i.e., it highlights more of the whole person, rather than only the sexual aspect. Others, however, have noted that "sexual orientation" is a more commonly used and easily recognized term, and that we should indeed focus on the key difference between straight and gay orientation. While in the previous edition of this Casebook I used "affectional orientation", in this edtion. I defer to those who offer the latter rationale.

Local and national policies recognize the importance of raising the awareness of and sensitivity to sexual orientation. Such policies are reflected in statements of the National Education Association, the National School Boards Association, the Child Welfare League of America, the American Academy of Pediatrics, the American Federation of Teachers, and the American Psychological Association (Horowitz & Loehnig, 2005). At the same time, throughout the nation, negative attitudes toward persons of differing sexual orientation linger.

As microcosms of society, schools often reflect matters of national interest. Issues such as gay marriage have brought increasing national attention to matters of sexual orientation. Whether teacher advocates are proactive in addressing such issues, or whether these issues are brought to the fore by students, matters of sexual orientation commonly arise in the school and classroom.

Chapter 8 introduces a number of real situations that may help elevate the dialogue regarding gay, lesbian, bisexual, and transgender (GLBT) issues. Inquiry into these cases may be aided by a more clear understanding of the following terms and concepts:

bisexual	lesbian
family	LGBT
gay	out
gender dyphoria	partner/significant other
GLBT	pink triangle
heterosexism	queer
heterosexual	questioning
heterosexual privilege	sexual orientation
homophobia	transgender
homosexual	transsexual
inclusive language	transvestite
internalized homophobia	xenophobia
intersexed individuals	

Definitions of key terms are included in the glossary of this text.

27

Not in My Group—He's Gay!

A student publicly objects to the inclusion of a classmate in his small group because, he claims, the classmate is "gay."

Ms. Collins was a firm believer in multicultural education that has the potential to lead to social reform. She organized her curriculum around issues of race, gender, class, disability, language, and sexual orientation. She used the lives of students in her classes as the starting point for addressing such issues.

On this day Ms. Collins' students were busily engaged in small-group discussions about their family heritage projects. She had asked students to share the information about their ethnic heritage that they had obtained from their parents or guardians the night before. Ms. Collins hoped that not only would the small-group discussions give her pupils opportunities to express themselves, but they might also help identify differences and similarities among classmates. Further, she thought the discussions would help them be more thoughtful about what else they would need to find out to make their projects more complete.

As she moved to the small group of students in the rear of the room, Xeng, a Hmong student new to the class, said to her as he pointed to a classmate named Kim, "I don't want him in my group. He's gay!" The other group members covered their mouths and laughed.

Ms. Collins was caught by surprise. Consistent enforcement of class rules established at the beginning of the school year had prevented the use of such labels in her class until today. She noticed that Kim appeared embarrassed by Xeng's comment.

"Do you know what 'gay' means?" she asked, in an effort to determine if Xeng was just repeating something he had heard someone else say, without knowing what it meant.

"Yes," replied Xeng. "It's when one man has sex with another man."

Ms. Collins was baffled. She thought to herself, "Should I ask if Xeng is sure that Kim is gay? Should I ask Xeng if he is angry with Kim, and, if so, why? Should I reprimand Xeng for making his judgment public? How should I respond to Kim?"

Ms. Collins was aware of the tremendous controversy over the inclusion in many schools of GLBT (gay, lesbian, bisexual, transgender) issues in the classroom. She would review the school policy and would discuss the matter with the principal.

Questions for Reflection

1. List possible factors that may have motivated Xeng to say what he said about Kim.
2. Write several sentences illustrating how you would respond to the students in this situation. Would you respond differently (a) if Xeng were not a new student, or (b) if Xeng had personal problems at home?
3. Knowing that the word "gay" is often used as a derogatory term, under what conditions, if any, would you involve the class in a discussion of this issue? Write down the actual opening statements/questions you would use to introduce such a discussion.
4. What other incidents regarding sexual orientation have you observed in schools? How were they addressed? How should they have been addressed?
5. What district and state policies and practices exist that relate to sexual orientation in the school, e.g., are there any statutes that require a safe environment for GLBT students?

Activities for Extending Thinking

1. Discuss with an experienced practicing teacher the strategies he or she uses to create and maintain a safe classroom environment for all students. List those strategies in writing and be prepared to share in class.
2. Interview an advocate for gay, lesbian, bisexual, and transgender students to identify key issues and specific strategies that classroom teachers can use to create a safe, inclusive environment.
3. Talk with a gay, lesbian, bisexual, or transgender student regarding classroom incidents experienced by him or her, or by friends who are GLBT. Elicit recommendations for preventing negative experiences and encouraging positive ones.
4. Discuss with a principal or superintendent the school and district policies regarding the inclusion of GLBT issues in his or her school(s).

In Islam, Homosexuality Is a Sin and a Crime

A student confides in her class that she is lesbian, and a Muslim student states that homosexuality is a sin and a crime in Islam.

Ms. Elness worked hard to develop an inclusive classroom. She believed in honoring cultural diversity, in designing multicultural curricula, and, in general, running a student-centered classroom. Because they knew she cared about all students, her pupils trusted her.

As part of her service to the school, Ms. Elness served as faculty sponsor of the Gay, Lesbian, Bisexual, Transgender (GLBT) support group that met bimonthly after school. She recalled that three years ago when she volunteered to sponsor the group, she had been nervous. Each year, however, her work as an advocate for students in the GLBT group had become more and more gratifying.

In addition to providing a forum for GLBT students to socialize and to discuss important issues, Ms. Elness would meet with other faculty to help them understand the general and specific needs of students in the group. Each year, on the first day of class, in her own classes she would discuss her work with the group so that students would know of her belief in the importance of creating a safe environment for all.

It was the sixth week of the school year. Ms. Elness had distributed newspapers and asked students to read and summarize for the class a news report of a current event. Tyrone reported an incident on a local university campus in which a number of students had harassed and physically beaten a student because he was gay.

Robert responded to the report, "I don't think that happens that much anymore. Most people are more accepting of people who are different."

Margie raised her hand. "I disagree," she said. "I'm a lesbian, and when people find out, they often look at me funny or avoid me entirely."

Ms. Elness was somewhat surprised. Margie had not confided in her, or as far as she knew in anyone else in the school, about her sexual orientation.

Before Ms. Elness could respond, Fahid, a Muslim student, said in a calm, informing tone of voice, "In many countries for Islamic believers, it is a sin and crime to practice homosexuality. Those who believe in Islam know they will be punished, even killed if they are found to be practicing homosexuality."

Ms. Elness sensed that Fahid was intending merely to describe a belief system held by Muslim people, not to promote a position or to demean Margie. At the same time, his comments seemed ill timed, for Margie had taken a risk to share her secret with the class, only to be informed that her disposition was considered a sin and a crime by a formidable group of people. Several students rolled their eyes, as if to suggest that Fahid was being intolerant in expressing a narrow point of view, and was out of line. Mark verbalized their dissatisfaction in a disgusted tone of voice: "That's only the opinion of one religion—it doesn't mean it actually is a sin or a crime—only that one religion thinks it is."

Jennifer cautioned Mark and the others who had rolled their eyes, "Let's remember now that Fahid is describing for us another cultural perspective. We ought not judge him for helping us to understand another point of view."

Noting that there was only a minute left in the period, Ms. Elness interrupted, "Yes, I appreciate the comments of both Margie and Fahid. And Jennifer is right—we must acknowledge the right of both Margie and Fahid to hold the beliefs that they hold." She had barely finished when the bell rang.

As the students filed out, she wondered, "How should I follow up with Fahid, Margie, Mark, and Jennifer? Should we follow up in class tomorrow, or go on with the next lesson in the unit plan?"

Questions for Reflection

1. In your opinion, how should Ms. Elness follow up with
   a. Margie?
   b. Fahid?
   c. Mark?
   d. Jennifer?
   e. the class?
   f. others? (identify)
2. Views opposing homosexuality are made clear by Fahid. What, if anything, should the teacher have done to represent the views of those who support it?
3. What assumptions had Mark made about Fahid's comments? Do they seem warranted?
4. What, if any, are the positive aspects of this case?
5. If you were the teacher, what might you have done differently to prevent, guide, or correct inappropriate student behaviors?

Activities for Extending Thinking

1. Discuss with a gay, lesbian, bisexual, or transgender student his or her P-12 school experience. Inquire about what the school is currently doing and what else, if anything, it could do to provide a safe, inclusive environment for GLBT students.
2. List specific steps you can take to better advocate for a safe environment for all students, particularly those who are GLBT or questioning.
3. Develop a list of curriculum resources that include gay, lesbian, bisexual, or transgendered persons and issues that could be used at the grade level at which you teach. Include several nonfiction and fiction resources.
4. Discuss with a school administrator (a principal, or superintendent) her or his school and district policies on GLBT issues.

Case 29

"Lesbian!": Responding to Name-Calling

A teacher considers ways to avoid sending the wrong message when responding to a name-calling incident.

Ms. Green's students were returning from lunch. The aide who had lunch duty popped her head in the classroom to give Ms. Green a "heads up" that a couple of students seemed to be having a disagreement. Ms. Green asked who the students were but before the aide could respond, two girls appeared at her desk. Sophia and Leyla told Ms. Green that Paul was teasing them during recess.

The two girls explained that they were walking around the playground talking and holding hands when Paul ran up behind them and started saying, "Lesbians! Lesbians!" The girls stated that they were not lesbians but were just friends, holding hands like they would hold hands with their mom or dad if they were on a walk with them.

This incident reminded Ms. Green of a news article she had read about a 7-year old student in another state who had told a classmate that his mother was gay. A teacher who overheard the remark scolded him, telling him that "gay" was a "bad" word. Further, the boy had to come to school early and repeatedly write: "I will never use the word 'gay' in school again." Ms. Green recalled that the American Civil Liberties Union (ACLU) demanded that the school apologize to the boy and his mother.

It was apparent to Ms. Green that this would be a sensitive subject to tackle. She wanted to be sure to communicate to the students that the act of teasing was not appropriate, but she did not want them to think that the word "lesbian" was a "bad" word, thus implying that persons who are lesbian are bad. She knew the whole class was waiting for a response and she had to reply with caution.

Questions for Reflection

1. Should the teacher in this situation simply treat the incident as a case of student behavior management (teasing), or should she in addition, address with the class the sexual orientation aspect of the incident? Give a brief rationale for your answer.
2. How can the teacher avoid sending the message that calling someone a lesbian is disrespectful and inappropriate without having them conclude that "lesbian" is an inappropriate lifestyle? Write 3–4 sentences representing your verbatim response to the name-calling incident.

3. In what situations have you heard someone use a term of sexual orientation as a means to degrade another?

4. How can a teacher set up the classroom ahead of time in order to avoid a situation like this?

5. Examine your own personal opinions about sexual orientation and reflect on how they may affect your own teaching process.

6. How could the teacher positively affect school policy regarding name calling and other GLBT issues?

Activities for Extending Thinking

1. Review and report research findings on the relation of rates of verbal abuse, assaults, depression, and suicide in adolescents of heterosexual and GLBT backgrounds.

2. Identify three or four local community resource centers that provide advocacy/support for students of GLBT orientation. Contact at least one of them and report on the nature and scope of their service, e.g., how many students do they serve, what is the racial/ethnic makeup of the constituency, etc. Include all contact information, e.g., phone number, e-mail address, and street address.

3. Develop an outline of a unit plan or a series of lesson plans in your own subject matter area that would help your students learn about GLBT needs, interests, and lifestyles.

4. The following possible response to homophobic remarks made by students is suggested by Alan Horowitz, a program specialist for the St. Paul Public Schools Out for Equity program:

   Name it: "That is homophobic harassment (or an age-appropriate alternative)."

   Claim it: "That is not permitted in this classroom (or school) because it is disrespectful."

   Stop it: "It won't happen again. If it does (state consequences)."

   Critique this response. Suggest changes, if any. Provide clear, age-appropriate alternative language for younger pupils. (From What to Say to "That's So Gay," by A. Horowitz, *Minnesota Educator*, p. 3, December 17, 2004.)

5. From the following sample book list, read one text and briefly describe how it could be integrated into your curriculum.

   Freymann-Weyr, G. (2002). *My Heartbeat*. New York: Penguin. As she tries to understand the closeness between her older brother and his best friend, 14-year-old Ellen finds her relationship with each of them changing.

   Hartinger, B. (2003). *Geography Club*. New York: HarperCollins. A group of gay and lesbian teenagers find mutual support when they form the "Geography Club" at their high school.

   Levithan, D. (2003). *Boy Meets Boy*. New York: Knopf. A story of a sophomore in a high school like no other: the cheerleaders ride Harleys, the homecoming queen used to be a guy named Daryl (she now prefers Infinite Darlene), and the gay–straight alliance was formed to help straight kids learn how to dance.

Matthews, A. (2003). *The Flip Side*. New York: Delacorte Press. Robert, a British 15-year-old, is confused when he plays the part of Rosalind while studying Shakespeare in school and discovers parts of his personality that he did not know existed.

Myracle, L. (2003). *Kissing Kate*. New York: Dutton. Sixteen-year-old Lissa's relationship with her best friend changes after they kiss at a party and Lissa does not know what to do, until she gets help from an unexpected new friend.

Peters, J. A. (2003). *Keeping You a Secret*. New York: Little, Brown. As she begins a very tough last semester of high school, Holland finds herself puzzled about her future and intrigued by a transfer student who wants to start a Lesbigay club at school.

Peters, J. A. (2004). *Luna*. New York: Little, Brown. Fifteen-year-old Regan's life, which has always revolved around keeping her older brother Liam's transsexuality a secret, changes when Liam decides to start the process of "transitioning" by first telling his family and friends that he is a girl who was born in a boy's body.

Sanchez, A. (2001). *Rainbow Boys*. New York: Simon & Schuster. Three high school seniors, a jock with a girlfriend and an alcoholic father, a closeted gay, and a flamboyant gay rights advocate, struggle with family issues, gay bashers, first sex, and conflicting feelings about each other.

Sanchez, A. (2003). *Rainbow High*. New York: Simon & Schuster. Sequel to *Rainbow Boys*. Follow three gay high school seniors as they struggle with issues of coming out, safe sex, homophobia, being in love, and college choices.

Taylor, W. (2003). *Pebble in a Pool*. Los Angeles: Alyson Books. Two popular high school students enter their senior year full of confidence. After a gruesome accident, the outpouring of grief in their school starkly contrasts with a decidedly more muted reaction to the gay-bashing murder of another student.

Winthrow, S. (2001). *Box Girl*. Toronto: Groundwood Books. Gwen's mother communicates with her, promising a reunion, through postcards with French stamps and no return address. Gwen plans to be a loner until she meets Clara.

Design Your Own Case

Sexual Orientation

Design a case that explores an issue of sexual orientation in the classroom. The story can focus on a method or strategy related to a single subject matter area (e.g., English or social studies) or on a more generic method or strategy pertinent to a wider range of subject matter areas. Your issue might also relate to:

- Planning and preparation
- Classroom environment
- Instruction
- Teacher responsibilities*

In selecting a topic, reflect on recent or current field experiences, personal experiences as a student, or accounts of real classroom incidents. Include some demographic data that tell a bit about the community, school, classroom, teacher, students, and curriculum. Include at least one problem for which there is no obvious solution. Use fictitious names of persons and schools to maintain confidentiality. Your case should be approximately two pages in length (typed, double-spaced) and should include three to four "Questions for Reflection," and one or two "Activities for Extending Thinking." Go to Resource C and use the form to design your own case.

*The four categories are from *Enhancing Professional Practice: A Framework for Teaching*, by C. Danielson, 1996, Alexandria. VA: Association for Supervision and Curriculum Development.

Readings for Extending Thinking

Bass, E., & Kaufman, K. (1996). *Free your mind: The book for gay, lesbian and bisexual youth—and their allies*. New York: HarperPerennial.

Berzon, B. (Ed.). (2001). *Positively gay: New approaches to gay and lesbian life*. Berkeley, CA: Celestial Arts.

Butler, K. L., & Byrne, T. J. (1992). Homophobia among preservice elementary teachers. *Journal of Health Education, 23*(6), 357–358.

Cowan, T. (1992). *Gay men and women who enriched the world*. Boston: Alyson.

Evans, K. (2002). *Negotiating the self: Identity, sexuality, and emotion in learning to teach*. New York: Routledge.

Harbeck, K. M. (Ed.). (1992). *Coming out of the classroom closet: Gay and lesbian students, teachers, and curricula*. Binghamton, NY: Haworth.

Herdt, G., & Boxer, A. (1993). *Children of horizons: How gay and lesbian teens are leading a new way out of the closet*. Boston: Beacon.

Horowitz, A., & Loehnig, G. (2005). Safe schools manual. St. Paul, MN: Out for Equity of the St. Paul Public Schools.

Hutchins, L., & Kaahumanu, L. (Eds.). (1991). *Bi any other name: Bisexual people speak out*. Boston: Alyson.

Jennings, K. (1994). *Becoming visible: A reader of gay and lesbian history for high school and college students*. Boston: Alyson.

Remafedi, G. (Ed.). (1994). *Death by denial: Studies of suicide in gay and lesbian teenagers*. Boston: Alyson.

The NEA's "Strengthening the Learning Environment: An Education Employee's Guide to Gay and Lesbian Issues." To order: 800-229-4200; www.nea.org/books.

Williams, K., Doyle, M., Taylor, B., & Ferguson, G. (1992). Addressing sexual orientation in a public high school. *Journal of School Health, 62*(4), 154–156.

Internet Sites for Extending Thinking

http://www.glsen.org
Site of national organization fighting to end anti-gay bias in K–12 schools.

http://www.pflag.org
Links to resources on relationships, anti-gay hate crimes; bibliography—by Parents, Families, and Friends of Lesbians and Gays.

http://www.project10.org
Provides educational assistance for GLBT and questioning youth in public school, including "Tips for Teachers" and "Tips for Administrators" sections.

http://www.safeschoolscoalition.org
Resources, including handouts and publications, for teachers, students, and others. Some site features are in both English and Spanish.

www.gayscäpe.com
A search tool for over 102,000 gay, lesbian, and bisexual Web sites, allowing searches by country or topic.

www.deafqueer.org
A national nonprofit resource and information center for, by and about the Deaf Lesbian, Gay, Bisexual, Transgender, Intersex, and Questioning communities.

www.ifge.org
The International Foundation for Gender Education advocates for freedom of expression of all people. The site has information on conferences, scholarships, and resources, including links to electronic sites, books, book reviews, and the like.

www.lamdalegal.org
Lambda Legal is a national organization committed to achieving full recognition of the civil rights of lesbians, gay men, bisexuals, transgender people, and those with HIV through impact litigation, education, and public policy work.

www.iglhrc.org
The site for the International Gay and Lesbian Human Rights Commission, whose mission is to secure the full enjoyment of the human rights of all people and communities subject to discrimination or abuse on the basis of sexual orientation or expression, gender identity or expression, and/or HIV status.

http://www.amnestyusa.org/outfront/index.do
The site of Amnesty International USA which works to end abuse of LGBT persons, and protect and promote human rights of LGBT people within the United Nations (UN) and other international governmental bodies.

http://glaad.org
The Gay and Lesbian Alliance Against Defamation, a national media organization whose
 mission is to encourage accurate, fair, and inclusive lesbian and gay images in all
 forms of media.

http://www.ellabakercenter.org
The Ella Baker Center for Civil Rights has programs and resources for mobilizing and
 challenging human rights abuses, advocating community based activism, and
 promoting policy reform.

http://www.alp.org
The Audre Lorde Project is a GLBT, Two Spirit, People of Color Center for community
 organizing focusing on the New York City area.

http://www.binetusa.org
BiNet USA is an organization which offers resources to help promote understanding of
 bisexuality.

http://www.ngltf.org
The National Gay and Lesbian Task Force is a leading organization supporting LGBT
 civil rights.

Chapter 9

Language

Introduction

Language is an integral part of culture and values, and as such, it has a profound impact on the daily lives of children and youth. Indeed, how teachers handle language issues will often affect the personal and cultural identity, as well as the academic success, of both native English speaking students and English language learners (ELL students).

With increasing immigration comes an increasing need to be aware of real classroom issues of language acquisition and use. Many large urban school districts report upward of 60 or more languages spoken in the schools.

A fundamental challenge for everyone, child or adult, is to understand other people's perspectives and expectations. Part of addressing this challenge is acknowledging that individuals whose cultures are different often have different rules for language use. The specific challenge for any educator is to adapt to diverse communicative needs and expectations in the classroom. This is no easy task. But it is a task that recognizes the crucial importance of effective communication. If it is left undone, the role of the teacher in enhancing the teaching and learning enterprise is substantially compromised (Garcia, 2002).

The following terms and concepts may help in discussing the cases in Chapter 9:

bilingual	English language learners (ELL)
bilingual programs	English as a Second Language
Black English vernacular/Ebonics	limited English proficiency (LEP)
culturally and linguistically diverse (CLD)	low-incidence population

Definitions of key terms are included in the glossary of this text.

Case | 30

You'll Need Both Black Vernacular and Standard English

A teacher considers varying opinions from colleagues regarding the acceptance of student use of Ebonics.

Mr. Drake had corrected the creative writing homework assignment from the previous day. He had wrestled with one particular paper written by Matt Williams, an African-American student who was new to the school. Mr. Drake was unsure how to handle Matt's use of Black English Vernacular (BEV). Throughout the paper were statements in which "be" was used as a finite verb, statements such as "He be happy," and "When they both be home, they usually be working around the house." And there were other differences in the use of grammar, differences such as using "done" to note that an action had been completed, as in "She done finished it"; the use of double or triple negatives, as in "They ain't got no car"; and the use of "f" for "th" as in "wif" for with.

At lunch Mr. Drake approached Ms. Grover, a trusted colleague in the classroom next to him. He showed her Matt's paper. Ms. Grover read several paragraphs and said, "If I were you, I'd tell him that if I accepted this form of language, he would never learn to operate in society—that he would be at a disadvantage when applying for jobs. Moreover, I'd tell him that Black English Vernacular is a deviation from correct, standard English." Mr. Drake thanked her for her advice.

Mr. Drake also shared his problem with Ms. Manning. He knew she was taking a continuing education course on sociolinguistics at a nearby college. She was interested in his dilemma.

"Would you like to hear a few lines about dialects from our course text?" she asked. Mr. Drake nodded affirmatively. Ms. Manning read from her textbook:

> The fact is, however, that standard English is only one variety among many, although a peculiarly important one. Linguistically speaking, it cannot even legitimately be considered better than other varieties. The scientific study of all language has convinced scholars that all languages, and correspondingly all dialects, are equally "good" as linguistic systems. All varieties of a language are structured, complex, rule-governed systems that are wholly adequate for their speakers. . . . There is nothing at all inherent in non-standard varieties that makes them inferior.

Any apparent inferiority is due only to their association with speakers from underprivileged, low-status groups.*

When she had finished reading, she told Mr. Drake of three students in her classes, each of whom used a different form of BEV. She explained to him that Amy, from New York, might say, for example, "Let's get ready to roll to the store," while Darnelle, a white student from Georgia, might say, "Let's be fiddin [fixing] to go to tha sto," and Dion, from Louisiana, would likely say, "We goin to make groceries." It was clear to Mr. Drake that Black English varied by region, depending on the cultural context in which it was learned and used.

Mr. Drake thanked Ms. Manning for her comments. On his way home from school, Mr. Drake wondered how he should respond to Matt's use of Black English in his paper.

Questions for Reflection

1. What other information, if any, would you need in order to decide how you would respond to Matt?
2. Write verbatim how you would begin a conversation with Matt about his use of BEV. Include specific comments about how his use of BEV will affect his grade on this assignment and on other work in your class in the future. Include elements of good feedback (i.e., it is specific, constructive, substantive, and accurate).
3. How might your response affect Matt's learning, his sense of self-worth, and the socio-emotional climate of your classroom?
4. What limits, if any, would you establish regarding the use of nonstandard English in your classroom?
5. How does the cultural context of the class, school, and community affect how you would respond to Matt?

Activity for Extending Thinking

1. Discuss with parents and teachers, including parents and teachers of color, the issue of allowing or encouraging the use of dialects in the classroom. Elicit their opinions regarding your policies and practices, as well as how flexible and responsive a teacher should be in accepting the use of dialects. Summarize your discussions in writing.

Socio linguistics: An Introduction to Language and Society, by P. Trudgill, 1984, New York: Penguin Books, p. 20.

Case | 31

They Speak English and Spanish Well, but a Learning Disability Creates Problems in Reading and Writing

A teacher and principal discuss programs and resources for two Hispanic students, each of whom has a learning disability and limited language proficiency.

Ms. Perez was regarded by students and colleagues as a hardworking and well-respected first-year teacher at Central. She loved kids and wanted them to enjoy learning. She was warm and compassionate, had a good sense of humor, and, at the same time, was clearly in charge of her classroom. She acted quickly and fairly when her young students needed guidance or correction. She spoke both English and Spanish fluently.

Ms. Perez was committed to designing lessons that were developmentally appropriate and that reflected the culturally diverse society in which her students would live. She learned quickly about the characteristics, needs, interests, and abilities of her students, and although she admitted to not having great knowledge about the many ethnicities, special abilities, and language acquisition needs of children, she worked hard at identifying resources that might supplement her knowledge.

Two of Ms. Perez's Hispanic students, Rita and Ramona, in their third year in an English-speaking school, possessed highly developed oral language skills in both English and Spanish, and a learning disability (LD) resulting in limited reading and writing abilities. Ms. Perez had made certain that the learning disability had been properly diagnosed, for she knew that academic English takes much longer than oral English to develop and that sometimes educators assume that any reading and writing problems are LD problems. Both of the girls had been similarly diagnosed in the Spanish-speaking school they had attended before coming to Central.

Ms. Perez aggressively supported a more holistic, student-centered collaborative approach in which the girls would be placed in a general education setting, experience an oral-based bilingual curriculum, and work on developing reading and writing in the content areas. Ms. Perez contacted special-service program personnel in bilingual and English as a Second Language (ESL) programs, special education, and counseling and worked with friends and colleagues to identify bilingual community members who could tutor the girls after school. She was indeed an advocate for culturally and linguistically diverse (CLD) students in her room.

It was in the fourth month of school when Ms. Perez had an idea that she felt needed to be discussed with the principal. One day during lunch break, she encountered Ms. Williams, the principal, in the cafeteria.

"Ms. Williams, I was wondering if it would benefit our staff and students if we were to offer some parent training programs that would improve parents' ability to help their children in reading, writing, and speaking," began Ms. Perez. "We could focus on practical interaction skills for building self-esteem and on positive approaches to learning to read and write. What do you think?"

"Sounds like a great idea!" replied Ms. Williams. "Mr. Lopez would have a lot to offer in the area of self-esteem and we could identify other Latino role models as speakers. We could also see if those who come to the first session or two would want to establish support groups—perhaps neighborhood based—to conduct ongoing discussions of our sessions and of personally relevant problems. I think it could work!"

"I think so, too," said Ms. Perez. "And perhaps later on there will be opportunities to encourage parent input on making curriculum more culturally relevant. It might be one good way of empowering parents."

"Let's bring it up at the next faculty meeting and see what we can do to move ahead. I'm all for it!" said Ms. Williams. She continued, "On a related topic, I've been wondering if Rita and Ramona should be moved to a self-contained classroom for learning-disabled students. They would be with students with similar needs and the instruction would be in English, the language in which they need the most work. What do you think?"

Ms. Perez had always thought that the current general education arrangement was the best for the two girls. At the same time, on other issues, she had usually agreed with Ms. Williams, whom she considered to be a wise administrator. She began to wonder: Would moving the girls from their current general education program into the special education class be good for them?

Questions for Reflection

1. What thoughts do you have about Ms. Perez's dilemma about a general versus special-education placement for Rita and Ramona?
2. How would you respond to the principal's proposal to move the girls to a self-contained special-education classroom? Provide a rationale for your response.
3. What other school and community resources for teachers would be helpful in dealing with CLD students?
4. What other school and community resources for CLD students would be helpful?
5. What suggestions would you have for modifying or expanding Ms. Perez's plan for a parent-education program?

Activities for Extending Thinking

1. Identify specific school and community resources available in a school in your area (perhaps a school in which you are currently involved in a field experience, or in which you are teaching) for CLD students and for students of other traditionally underrepresented groups.

2. Identify language and cultural-related parent-education programs in a local school (perhaps a school in which you are in a field experience or in which you are teaching). Briefly describe their goals, methods, and evidence of progress toward their goals.

3. Identify and interpret legal aspects of bilingual and special education, including major civil rights legislation, the Bilingual Education Act (also known as Title VII), the Individuals with Disabilities Education Act of 1990, and related case law.

4. On the Internet, explore state resources (e.g., state departments of education) and national resources for teachers and for students (e.g., U.S. Department of Education: www.ed.gov/index.html) that would serve you in curriculum planning in the future. Develop a list of other Web sites, such as Administration for Children and Families (www.acf.dhhs.gov). Identify and explore other such general sites as well as those more specific to the instruction of CLD students. (Because URLs are subject to change, be prepared to search for the organizations themselves.)

5. Participate in an education listserv and/or newsgroup such as edweb.cnidr.org: 90/usenets.html. Keep a journal of your participation.

6. Interview a parent of a CLD student to ascertain his or her views on how the school can provide better services for CDL children.

A Bilingual Teacher's Aide Assesses His New School

A bilingual teacher's aide ponders specific strategies for helping teachers better understand their ELL and bilingual students' abilities, interests, prior knowledge, and individual needs.

It was the first day of school and Andy Seng, a bilingual teacher's aide with 10 years of experience, entered his new school building. He was excited to meet the staff and students.

He had been pleased when he attended the workshop week prior to the first week of actual classes. He had seen "welcome" signs in several different languages posted above the doors. He had been greeted by bilingual volunteers, some of whom were students and some of whom were community members. He had noticed universal symbols and photos over important places, such as the bathrooms, cafeteria, library, and school office. He had also seen that many of the classrooms contained resource books in a number of different languages, and he had talked to teachers who said that they encouraged journal writing in the student's first language. All of these factors, he thought, would help to develop a positive atmosphere for English Language Learners (ELL) and bilingual students.

He and the principal had decided during workshop week that it might be useful for him to shadow one or two ELL students during the first day to get an idea of school and classroom policies and practices relative to ELL and bilingual pupils. On his first day, he followed two Vietnamese students, one throughout the morning, the other during the afternoon. Both had been placed in mainstreamed classrooms taught only in English.

At the end of each half day, he spoke with each student. "How did you like your morning?" he asked the first student, whose name was Hung. "It was confusing," Hung replied. "My teacher had the class work in small groups. Since I didn't know what to do, I just watched the other students. And later on the playground, the teacher had us play softball. She thought we'd all know how, but I had never heard of softball before. I was embarrassed."

When Andy asked Chau, the student he followed during the afternoon, Chau responded, "I think my teacher thinks I'm not as smart as the others. He gave me problems that were much more simple than those he gave to the other students." Chau paused. "After class some of the kids made fun of the lunch I brought from home—that made me feel bad." Andy had worked as a teacher's aide for five years in each of two other schools. He knew that most teachers accepted, appreciated, and supported ELL and bilingual students. However, he had also seen a few teachers who had expectations that were either much too low or much too high for such students. Most cases of too-high expectations involved students of Asian heritage; cases of too-low expectations usually involved Latino or African-American students. Based on his past experience, then, Chau's situation was an exception to the rule. Andy thanked both Hung and Chau for their responses and promised both of them that he would support them and other ELL and bilingual students throughout the term.

After school that day, Andy pondered ways that he might help teachers know more about the abilities, interests, and needs of each of their ELL and bilingual students. He knew that just telling teachers in a memo or even personally would not necessarily result in their knowing students better. He knew his goal was to be an advocate for students; now he just had to identify the strategies.

Questions for Reflection

1. Andy noted some positive steps the school and some individual teachers had taken to make students of other cultures feel more at home. What were they? What else could the school have done?
2. The students also mentioned some teacher behaviors that had a detrimental effect on student morale. What behaviors did they note? What would you have done differently in each case?

Teacher behaviors with detrimental effects	What I would have done
a.	a.
b.	b.
c.	c.

3. What kinds of information should teachers have about students in their classes? From what sources could they obtain each type of information?
4. Consider a school situation involving two students of another culture or of two different cultures—for example, two Russian students, or a Muslim and an Arab student, or a Native American and a Hispanic student. What cultural conflicts might arise?
5. What actions would you recommend that Andy take to address the problems he has encountered with Hung's and Chau's teachers? What cultural attributes must be taken into account when making these recommendations?

Activities for Extending Thinking

1. Discuss with officials of a local school the language diversity within that school. List the different languages spoken and the services for students who speak them. Include bilingual, ELL, and limited English-proficiency (LEP) services and programs.
2. Talk with a bilingual and an ELL teacher to identify methods they use to promote academic learning and language development in their classrooms. Discuss what regular-education teachers can do to help ELL, bilingual, and LEP students achieve their course goals.
3. Talk with an ELL teacher about how to address issues of working in groups, accessing prior knowledge, accommodating different learning styles, and assessment as they pertain to LEP students. Summarize your key insights in writing (one to two pages).

Computers and Culturally Diverse Learners

A teacher considers ways in which she can integrate computer technologies and cultural and individual preferences to more effectively meet the socioemotional and academic needs of her students.

Ms. Wright was pleased that for each of the past five years, the school had significantly increased the number of computers and software programs available to students. She believed, however, that neither computers nor software were culturally neutral, that they reflect the assumptions, expectations, and learning styles of their creators (usually White and male), and so she constantly looked for ways to integrate computer culture with the culture of individual students and the culture of the classroom.

To improve cross-cultural skills and intercultural understandings, Ms. Wright had developed an ongoing activity in which each of her students identified and communicated with a pen pal from another country. She was pleased that her classes were enthusiastic about using telecommunications technology to learn about the beliefs, behaviors, and values of persons of other cultures.

In activities involving research on the Internet, Ms. Wright encouraged multidirectional learning. She was as eager to learn from students as she was to have them learn from her. In addition, she encouraged students to help one another whenever possible.

Ms. Wright made every attempt to use computer technology to support a variety of individual and cultural differences. For example, she used visual and graphic representations preferred by some Native American students as a way of understanding; she established pairs and trios at computers as a way to meet the preference for cooperative learning of many Black, Asian, and Hispanic students; and she provided an overview and review of material, thereby adding a more global, less fragmented view preferred by many of her culturally diverse students. In each of her classes, Ms. Wright had several limited English proficiency (LEP) students of Russian, Croatian, and Puerto Rican heritage. While her LEP students had demonstrated remarkable adaptability, their limited English proficiency kept them a bit behind the other students in learning course content. To accommodate her LEP students' need to learn English, Ms. Wright would often allocate the last 15 minutes of class for the LEP students to complete computer drill-and-practice programs on English grammar, usage, and punctuation. During this same time, non-LEP students would engage in enrichment computer programs requiring creative problem solving in the course content. Ms. Wright believed that this was the best way to attend to the particular needs of both groups of students. By the fifth week of the term, Juan and Vicki, two of her LEP students, had politely reported that the grammar and usage worksheets on the computer were "boring." "We are learning some English, I guess," said Juan, "But I get tired of doing the same thing almost every day."

Ms. Wright replied, "I think that using technology to help me meet the differing needs of two groups of students is effective and efficient. This way I'm able to help you as well as the other students."

Juan and Vicki appeared unconvinced.

Questions for Reflection

1. What do you consider to be the strengths of Ms. Wright's attempts to use a variety of software programs to address the different learning styles of her diverse student body?
2. What would you change, if anything, about her approach?
3. Identify other cultural differences in styles of learning. How can educational computing technologies help address these cultural differences in learning?
4. What biases might be inherent in computer and related technologies? How would you adapt your approach to using computer technologies so as to eliminate such biases?
5. What other issues must teachers confront in order to achieve technology equity in their classrooms? For each issue identified, suggest a promising strategy, technique, or approach for addressing the issue.

Activities for Extending Thinking

1. Discuss with female students and students of color their assessment of the degree to which software on the Internet, on disk, and on CD-ROM is bias free and compatible with their styles of learning. Summarize key findings in writing.
2. Design a classroom activity in which students question software developers (programmers and designers) about the degree to which their products address cultural differences in users. Summarize your findings in writing.

Design Your Own Case

Language

Design a case that explores an issue of language diversity in the classroom. The story can focus on a method or strategy related to a single subject matter area (e.g., English or social studies) or on a more generic method or strategy pertinent to a wider range of subject matter areas. Your issue might also relate to:

- Planning and preparation
- Classroom environment
- Instruction
- Teacher responsibilities*

In selecting a topic, reflect on recent or current field experiences, personal experiences as a student, or accounts of real classroom incidents. Include some demographic data that tell a bit about the community, school, classroom, teacher, students, and curriculum. Include at least one problem for which there is no obvious solution. Use fictitious names of persons and schools to maintain confidentiality. Your case should be approximately two pages in length (typed, double-spaced) and should include three to four "Questions for Reflection," and one or two "Activities for Extending Thinking." Go to Resource C and use the form to design your own case.

*The four categories are from *Enhancing Professional Practice: A Framework for Teaching*, by C. Danielson, 1996, Alexandria, VA: Association for Supervision and Curriculum Development.

Readings for Extending Thinking

Artiles, A. J., & Trent, S. C. (1994). Overrepresentation of minority students in special education: A continuing debate. *Journal of Special Education, 27,* 410–437.

Baca, L. M., & Cervantes, H. T. (1989). *The bilingual special education interface* (2nd ed.). Upper Saddle River, NJ: Merrill/Prentice Hall.

Brinton, D., Goodwin, J., & Ranks, L. (1994). Helping language minority students read and write analytically: The journey into, through, and beyond. In F. Peitzman & G. Gadda (Eds.), *With different eyes* (pp. 57–88). Reading, MA: Addison Wesley Longman.

California Department of Education. (1990). *Bilingual education handbook: Designing instruction for LEP students.* Sacramento: Author.

Chan, J., & Chips, B. (1989). Helping LEP students survive in the content-area classroom. *Thrust, 18*(6), 49–51.

Clark, K. (1999). *From primary language instruction to English immersion: How five California districts made the switch.* Washington, DC: READ (Institute for Research in English Acquisition and Development).

Cummins, J. (1994). From coercive to collaborative relations of power in the teaching of literacy. In R. M. Ferdman, R. M. Weber, & A. G. Ramírez (Eds.), *Literacy across languages and cultures* (pp. 3–29). Albany: State University of New York Press.

Cummins, J. (1996). Primary language instruction and the education of language minority students. In *Schooling and language minority students: A theoretical framework* (2nd ed., pp. 3–46). Los Angeles: Evaluation, Dissemination and Assessment Center, School of Education, California State University, Los Angeles.

Cummins, J. (1999). Alternative paradigms in bilingual education research: Does theory have a place? *Educational Researcher, 28*(7), 26–34.

Cummins, J. (2000). Beyond adversarial discourse: Searching for common ground in the education of bilingual students. In C. J. Ovando & P. McLaren (Eds.), *The politics of multiculturalism and bilingual education: Students and teachers caught in the cross fire* (pp. 126–147). Boston: McGraw-Hill.

Delgado-Gaitan, C., & Trueba, H. (1991). *Crossing cultural borders.* New York: Falmer Press.

Díaz, S., Moll, L. C., & Mehan, H. (1996). Sociocultural resources in instruction: A context-specific approach. In *Beyond language: Social and cultural factors in schooling language minority students* (pp. 187–230). Los Angeles: Evaluation, Dissemination and Assessment Center, School of Education, California State University, Los Angeles.

Díaz-Soto, L. (1991). Understanding bilingual/bicultural young children. *Young Children, 46*(2), 30–36.

Ferdman, B. M., & Weber, R. M. (1994). Literacy across languages and cultures. In B. M. Ferdman, R. M. Weber, & A. G. Ramírez (Eds.), *Literacy across languages and cultures* (pp. 3–29). Albany, NY: State University of New York Press.

Gándara, P., Maxwell-Jolly, J., García, E., Asato, J., Gutiérrez, K., Stritkus, T., & Curry, J. (2000). *The initial impact of Proposition 227 on the instruction of English learners.* Davis, CA: University of California Linguistic Minority Research Institute.

Garcia, E. (2002). *Student cultural diversity: Understanding and meeting the challenge* (3rd ed.). New York: Houghton Mifflin.

Garcia, E. (2005). *Teaching and learning in two languages: Bilingualism and schooling in the United States.* New York: Teachers College Press.

Gersten, R. (1999). The changing face of bilingual education. *Educational Leadership, 56*(7), 41–45.

Gonzales, V., Brusca-Vega, R., & Yaukey, T. (1997). *Assessment and instruction of culturally and linguistically diverse students.* Boston: Allyn & Bacon.

Gottlieb, J., & Alter, M. (1995). *Overrepresentation of children of color referred to special education.* New York: New York University Department of Teaching Learning.

Griego-Jones, T. (1991). Rethinking programs for language minority students. *Journal of Educational Issues of Language Minority Students, 9,* 61–74.

Gunderson, L. (1991). *ESL literacy instruction: A guidebook to theory and practice.* Englewood Cliffs, NJ: Regents/Prentice Hall.

Hughes, A. (2003). *Testing for language teachers.* New York: Cambridge University Press.

Joyce, B. (Ed.). (1990). *Changing school culture through staff development.* Alexandria, VA: Association for Supervision and Curriculum Development.

Kuhlman, N., & Murray, D. E. (2000). Changing populations, changing needs in teacher preparation. In M. A. Snow (Ed.), *Implementing the ESL standards for pre-K–12 students through teacher education* (pp. 33–48). Alexandria, VA: Teachers of Speakers of Other Languages.

MacSwan, J. (2000). The Threshold hypothesis, semilingualism, and other contributions to a deficit view of linguistic minorities. *Hispanic Journal of Behavior Sciences, 20*(1), 3–45.

Minami, M., & Ovando, C. J. (2004). Language issues in multicultural contexts. In J. A. Banks & C. A. M. Banks (Eds.), *Handbook of research on multicultural education* (2nd ed., pp. 567–588), San Francisco: Jossey-Bass.

Moegher, M. E. (1995, October). Learning English on the Internet. *Educational Leadership, 53*(2), 88–90.

National Council for Languages and International Studies. (2004). *Language competence and cultural awareness in the United States*. Pamphlet. Washington, DC: Author.

National Forum on Personnel Needs for Districts with Changing Demographics. (1990, May). *Staffing the multilingually impacted schools of the 1990s*. Washington, DC: U.S. Department of Education.

Nielsen, D. (1998). *Second language acquisition and its effects on the social and emotional development of immigrant teens in a small midwestern middle school*. Unpublished doctoral dissertation. University of Nebraska, Lincoln.

Nieto, S. (1992). *Affirming diversity: The sociopolitical context of multicultural education*. New York: Longman.

OELA (Office of English Language Acquisition). (2004a). National Clearinghouse for English Language Acquisition and Language Instruction Education Programs. Retrieved August 8, 2004, from www.NCELA.gwu.edu.

Ogbu, J. U. (1999). Beyond language: Ebonics, proper English, and identity in a Black-American speech community. *American Educational Research Journal, 36*(2), 147–184.

Ovando, C., Collier, P., & Coombs, M. C. (2003). *Bilingual and ESL classrooms: Teaching in multicultural contexts* (3rd ed.). New York: McGraw-Hill.

Ovando, C. J., & McLaren, P. (2000). *The politics of multiculturalism and bilingual education: Students and teachers caught in the cross fire*. Boston: McGraw-Hill.

Peregoy, S. F., & Boyle, O. F. (1993). *Reading, writing, and learning in ESL*. Reading, MA: Addison Wesley Longman.

Porter, R. P. (1999–2000). The benefits of English immersion. *Educational Leadership, 57*(4), 52–56.

Smitherman, G., and Villanueva, V. (2003). Language diversity in the classroom: From intention to practice. Carbondale: Southern University Press.

Smitherman, G. (1999). *Talkin that talk: Language, culture, and education in African America*. New York: Routledge.

Snow, M. A. (Ed.). (2000). *Implementing the ESL standards for pre-K–12 students through teacher education*. Alexandria, VA: Teachers of Speakers of Other Languages.

Todd, L. (1997). Ebonics: An evaluation. *English Today, 13*, 13–17.

U.S. English, Inc. (2004, August). States with Official English Laws. Retrieved August 27, 2004, from www.us-english.org.

Internet Sites for Extending Thinking

http://members.aol.com/jakajk/ESLLessons.html
Classroom resources and materials.

http://www.eslpartyland.com
Lesson plans, quizzes, discussion forums, and other engaging resources.

http://www.eltweb.com/liason/
A well-organized index of resources including "Bilingual Education", "Immigration", and "Multicultural Issues".

http://www.cal.org/ericcll/digest/ncrcds04.html
Outline pedagogical principles to guide teachers of second language learning students. (National Center for Research on Cultural Diversity and Second Language Learning, for ERIC Digest).

Chapter 10

Ageism

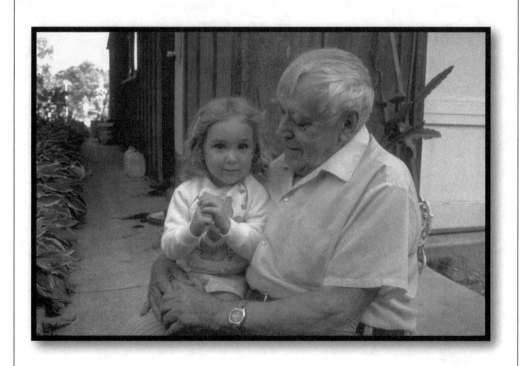

Introduction

Ageism, or bias based on age, involves stereotypical thinking (usually negative) of persons of a particular age group. The two most commonly targeted are (1) adolescents and (2) the elderly. Children and adolescents face many challenges, including neglect, child abuse, substance abuse, anxiety, depression and suicide, poverty, sexual behavior issues, and violence, to name a few. Each of these challenges should be viewed and addressed through a lens of race, ethnicity, sexual orientation, language, religion, special needs, and/or gender.

In addition to working through their own age-related issues, children and adolescents develop thoughts, opinions, and values related to persons in other age groups. For example, they may come to view middle-aged or elderly persons in a positive or negative light. Teachers can assist in helping to develop healthy attitudes toward persons of all age groups.

The cases in this section are designed to provide examples of age-related issues that may be purposely included in curriculum, or that may occur spontaneously in the classroom. Terms and concepts that may be helpful in analyzing the cases include:

aged	elderly
ageism	harassment
bullying	stages of development
child abuse	youth-oriented culture

Definitions of key terms are located in the glossary of this text.

Age as a Factor in Bullying and "Cyberbullying"

A teacher responds to instances of older students harassing younger students.

"Word has it that peer mediation has solved your problem with the older girls on the volleyball team—is that true?" Ms. Wheeler asked Tanisha, a younger and new member of the team. "Yep—I guess. As long as Becky and Liz keep their end of the bargain. They're not to pick on me and my friends anymore, just 'cause we're new to the team and just 'cause they're older." "I'm glad to hear you've agreed to get along," said Ms. Wheeler.

Ms. Wheeler knew both the older and the younger group of girls. Each group was diverse in many ways, including race, ethnicity, socioeconomic status, and language. Hence, she had concluded that the key factor in this conflict between the groups was age. Ms. Wheeler knew that the harassment had been extended beyond school hours through the use of the Internet. She knew all too well that e-mail messages and Web logs enabled intimidating messages to be more humiliating, as gossip, ugly epithets, and even embarrassing pictures are circulated more widely, and are less apparent to adults.

In fact, she had recalled in talking with the school psychologist about "cyberbullying" that several factors—the distance between the bully and the victim, the typical lack of impulse control of young students, and underdeveloped empathy skills—seemed to converge, often resulting in particularly brutal harassment. The psychologist had shared knowledge of cases at other schools in which students had been identified as "sexually active," "boring," "racist," and the like, and of an instance where a young male student had made a video of himself singing to a girl he liked, who immediately posted it all over the Internet. Cell phones with photo and video capabilities brought a similar set of potential problems.

Ms. Wheeler recalled too that when she had taught another grade level, similar harassment problems had occurred, albeit with two groups of boys. In those situations too, each group had noticeable diversity except for age. Age seemed to be a factor in a number of situations of which she was familiar.

Questions for Reflection

1. Identify issues or conflicts that you've experienced as a student that may be age related. What teacher behavior may help prevent such conflicts?

   Conflict or Issue   Teacher Preventative

   a.

   b.

2. Once age-related conflicts have occurred, what conflict mediation strategies might you recommend for addressing each issue? Integrate research on best practice as you respond to this question.

   Conflict   Response

   a.

   b.

   c.

3. Think about question #2 in terms of technology-related issues, e.g., Internet, cell phones, video technologies. Identify conflicts and responses that you know about or that you can imagine.

   Conflict   Response

   a.

   b.

   c.

4. In your subject matter, identify resources, e.g., children's or adolescent literature sources, videos/DVDs, etc., that could be used to support lessons that deal with age. (Topics may include early or middle childhood, adolescent development, drug use, anxiety, depression and suicide, dating, and others.)

   Resources for Students

   a.

   b.

   c.

   d.

   e.

5. How important is it to help students think about issues related to age—issues such as age stereotyping, sexual harassment, drug and alcohol use, anxiety, depression and suicide, bullying/"cyberbullying," and care for the aged? Which of these and what other topics would you be able to address in your subject matter area?

Subject Matter Area	Topic
a.	
b.	
c.	

Activities for Extending Thinking

1. Using professional standards from teacher education or standards from your subject matter area, outline (on one page) general ideas for a project on an age-related issue that you could assign in a class that you will likely teach.

   Identify several Internet sites that deal with an age-related issue and provide a one-paragraph description of each site. Identify two to three print resources and two to three videos or DVDs (media products) that appear to be appropriate for your project and provide a one-paragraph description of each.

Internet Site	Description
a.	
b.	
c.	

Print Resource	Description
a.	
b.	

Media Resource	Description
a.	
b.	

2. Discuss with local school officials steps they have taken or steps they feel should be taken to prevent technology-related harassment among students, both during and after school hours. Include interview questions related to developing a positive classroom/school climate, student and staff training, support of the victims, identification of and consequences for bullies and related issues. List steps taken and those that they would recommend.

   a. Steps taken

      1.

      2.

   b. Steps they would recommend

      1.

      2.

The Wages We Will Get as Adults Will Pay for the Elderly? What's Up with That?

A lesson on Social Security causes students to wonder why they must pay for someone else's support.

"You say that when we are working the government will take money from our wages to pay for the care of old people? That's not fair! Why don't their wages cover them and ours cover us? If we work for it, we should get it when we're older!" asserted Dominique. Several others added their usual "yeah, what's the deal?" A final somewhat muffled comment came from the back of the room—"Yeah, what the f_ _ _."

Mrs. Bonds replied, "You know the generation of folks behind you will contribute a part of their wages to support you when you are older. So in that way, everyone wins, right?"

"I'd rather not support people I don't even know. And how do we know they won't change the system by the time we're old—maybe we won't get anything," chimed Michael.

Mrs. Bonds recognized the "what's in it for me?" orientation of her students. She thought to herself—the third stage of moral reasoning—OK, we can work with that.

Mrs. Bonds altered her approach. "Actually your grandparents, parents, and their friends as well as some of your neighbors are in the group that you'll support. Does that make a difference? Would you be more willing to support relatives through Social Security?"

The class was quiet for a moment—they seemed to be considering Mrs. Bonds' comment.

"Well, if I knew my money was going for *their* care, I guess it'd be OK," replied Juan.

"Yeah," said Mai, "my folks and grandparents deserve good care and I'd be happy to contribute."

Questions for Reflection

1. Should Mrs. Bonds have expanded the discussion of social/cultural values of the aged? Why or why not?
2. What additional questions or comments could Mrs. Bonds have made to expand student thinking about societal values regarding care for the aged?

3. What lessons could you design in your subject matter area that would help students consider social/cultural attitudes and/or values on aging?
4. List two to three alternative responses that a teacher could use in responding to profanity such as expressed in this case. Each response should represent a slightly different approach and/or draw on a variety of strategies for addressing the issue of profanity in the classroom.

Activities for Extending Thinking

1. Outline requirements/guidelines for a P–12 student project that involves student interviews of older members of your culture regarding the care of the elderly. Specify a general interview topic and write out three to four sample interview questions on that topic. Identify two to three student resources for students to examine.
2. Outline requirements for a P–12 student project similar to that in activity #1, but which involves age-related practices of members of a culture other than that of the students' own.

You're Teaching Our Kids to Disrespect the Elderly?

Parents misinterpret a teacher's lesson on age and culture.

"I understand you taught a lesson last Friday in which you suggested that the elderly are of little value to anyone — that they can be disregarded—indeed *should* be disregarded in certain situations," asserted a parent on the phone.

The teacher, Ms. Rice was stunned. "No, honestly, I would never do that," she replied. "The lesson was about certain groups of nomadic Eskimos who often travel great distances with limited supplies of food. It's a fact that when faced with only enough food left to feed part of the group, that it was understood as a cultural norm, that the oldest would volunteer to be left in the wilderness to perish. We did not suggest that in our culture we should also follow that practice. In fact, a number of students stated how gratifying it was to know that our culture does so much to provide for the elderly with nursing homes, in-home care, and other support for the elderly. In the final analysis, I feel that there was unanimous agreement that we should continue and even expand the resources to provide for our aged," explained Ms. Rice.

"I doubt if that point got across to many of the students," replied Ms. Carroll. "The way my son stated it was, 'If you have to make such hard decisions, the Eskimos have a good point—favor the young who have more strength to continue and ensure the survival of the species.' That's not promoting the welfare of the older citizens, is it? Why even bring up the survival problems of nomadic people? That'll never happen to us," complained the caller.

"I feel students need to understand the dilemmas, customs, and values of other cultures. Moreover, wrestling with moral dilemmas helps them clarify their own thinking about such important issues. Perhaps some day they'll advocate expanded care for the aged."

"Well, I don't like it and neither do the other parents I've talked to. We don't want you planting seeds that are contrary to our beliefs. We're contacting Principal Hunter to have this curriculum modified. I'll ask that she have you drop any materials and all lessons that may mislead students regarding social values on aging."

After the phone conversation, Ms. Rice reflected on the surprising call. She recalled that in previous years, student evaluations forms had high ratings for the set of lessons on Eskimo culture. She remembered that in addition, a number of students had told her that the readings and discussion had really made them think and that they felt they and the class had more compassion for people—especially older people as a result of their study. She headed for her evaluation file to gather the data she'd need to support her case with the principal.

Questions for Reflection

1. Might there have been steps Ms. Rice could have taken to prevent such parent misunderstanding?
2. What should she do now that a number of parents have misunderstood her intent?
3. What lessons in your subject matter area(s) might be useful lessons on culture and age? List three potential lesson topics.

Subject Matter Area	Lesson Topics
a.	a.
b.	b.
c.	c.

Activities for Extending Thinking

1. Design a student project in your subject matter area in which P–12 students research how age relates to another diversity area, e.g., race, gender, religion, etc. Provide two to three project goals and two to three activity ideas in outline form.
2. Identify commonly held stereotypes of teenagers.

    a.   d.

    b.   e.

    c.   f.

    List ways you as a teacher could counter these stereotypes in a course that you may teach.
3. Identify commonly held stereotypes of the elderly (those over 70 years of age).

    a.   d.

    b.   e.

    c.   f.

    List ways you as a teacher could counter these stereotypes in a course that you might teach.

Age-Related Cultural Needs of Children and Youth

A teacher reflects on the various age-related needs of her students, and wonders which needs might be culturally based.

It was the middle of fall term, the time of year that Ms. Middleton usually assessed the degree to which she had been meeting her students' needs. At the beginning of the year she had reviewed her personal collection of teacher education materials and had identified what she felt were the most prevalent cognitive, emotional, physical, social, and moral needs of her students. She had checked various developmental theories, in an attempt to identify the stages at which her students might be operating, always keeping in mind that some students may be at a different stage than that of most students of a particular age. Just this morning she had told her student teacher: "I've found developmental theories to be helpful in predicting the usual stages and behaviors of students, but I also have known individuals who were exceptions to what the theories predict."

Her students did, indeed, seem to fit the profiles suggested by scholars. She observed physical changes in size and strength; cognitive changes in ability to do some abstract thinking, question adult values, and increased daydreaming; and socioemotional shifts including increased sensitivity to criticism, moodiness, heightened self-consciousness, disturbances in self-esteem, and the need for both privacy and, at the same time, the need to be understood. She had also seen social needs in play, such as the increase in peer influence and the strong need for peer relationships. Furthermore, Ms. Middleton sensed the interaction of these age-related changes with other diversity areas such as race, ethnicity, gender, and the like. She believed, for instance, that members of target groups, such as students of color, of a GLBT orientation, and so on, would have experienced the same types of criticism experienced by White, straight students, as well as criticism related to their race and/or gender orientation group membership. Such additional negativity would certainly tend to lead to lower self-esteem, with concomitant reduction in motivation, and academic and social success.

When Ms. Middleton thought about cultural needs of students, she thought first of general notions about target groups, or as she often thought of them, as "microcultures." Her impression was that members of microcultures often tend to be more group (e.g., family, neighborhood) oriented, more cooperative (versus competitive), and more relationship or socially oriented. She thought for example of many of her Hispanic/Latino students who came to school expecting shows of affection from teachers like those they experienced at home.

In addition to the general cultural needs about which she needed to know, Ms. Middleton sought to learn more specifics about age-related cultural needs of her students. For example, on this Monday morning in October, she had asked her students: "What cultural history, heritage, or culture do you feel you want or need to know more about?"

Marcela replied: "I would like to do a project on contributions of Hispanic/Latino people to the history and culture of the United States of America." Gloria, stated: "I would like to identify positive models representing my Japanese heritage." Others gave similar responses related to learning about their cultural heritage. Even White students wanted to learn more about their distinct cultural origins and the contributions that their ethnic groups have made to society.

The comments from the students seemed to correspond to the work of a scholar (Manning, 2000) whose workshop she had attended recently. At that workshop, three culturally-related developmental characteristics were identified. First, young adolescents form cultural identities; second, they form close friends, social networks, and opinions of the similarities and differences of others; and third, they develop a sense of justice and fairness related to how people should be treated. Ms. Middleton pondered, "How can I be developmentally and culturally responsive to my students?"

Questions for Reflection

1. Identify four to five multicultural educational experiences that the teacher in this story can use to meet the cultural and developmental needs of her young adolescent students.
2. Considering the age of the students you hope to teach (or do teach), what developmental needs do they have in general? (You may want to use the groupings of K–3, 4–6, 7–9, and 10–12, or similar groupings.)
3. What more specific culturally-related developmental needs do they possess? For example, if you anticipate teaching students of African-American descent, what age-related needs do you expect them to have, and how might you address those needs?

Activities for Extending Thinking

1. Discuss the issues in this case and the "Questions for Reflection" above with K–12 students. Summarize your findings in writing.
2. Explore the work of other scholars on cultural/developmental needs of students. Summarize your findings in writing.
3. Discuss with other experienced teachers and/or administrators, the issues in this case. Summarize your findings in writing.

Design Your Own Case

Ageism

Design a case that would help classmates explore issues related to diversity in age. The story can focus on a method or strategy related to a single subject matter area (e.g., English or social studies) or on a more generic method or strategy pertinent to a wider range of subject matter areas. Your issue might also relate to:

- Planning and preparation
- Classroom environment
- Instruction
- Teacher responsibilities*

In selecting a topic, reflect on recent or current field experiences, personal experiences as a student, or accounts of real classroom incidents. Include some demographic data that tell a bit about the community, school, classroom, teacher, students, and curriculum. Include at least one problem for which there is no obvious answer. Use fictitious names of persons and schools to maintain confidentiality. Your case should be approximately two pages in length (typed, double-spaced) and should include three to four "Questions for Reflection," and one or two "Activities for Extending Thinking." Go to Resource C and use the form to design your own case.

*The four categories are from *Enhancing Professional Practice: A Framework for Teaching*, by C. Danielson, 1996, Alexandria, VA: Association for Supervision and Curriculum Development.

Readings for Extending Thinking

Allen, S. D., Runell, M., Varghese, R., Williams, T. O., Adams, M., & Whitlock, E. R. (2004). Review of the Year's Publications for 2003: Social Justice Education. *Equity & Excellence in Education, 37*(4).

Brown, H. (2003). Schools take on studies of child labor. *Education Week, 22*(31), 1–14.

Crawford, P. A. (2000). Crossing boundaries: Addressing ageism through children's books. *Reading Horizons, 40*(3), 161–174.

Edwards, C. H. (2005). *Teaching and learning in middle and secondary schools.* Upper Saddle River, NJ: Pearson Merrill/Prentice Hall.

Forman, B. I. (1985). Addressing ageism in the schools. *Curriculum Review, 25*, 10–12.

Fried, S. B., & Mehrotra, C. M. (2000). *Teaching diversity and aging through active learning strategies: An annotated bibliography.*

Gullette M. M. (2004). Aged by culture. Chicago: University of Chicago Press.

Jakobi, P. (1999). Using the World Wide Web as a teaching tool: Analyzing images of aging and the visual needs of an aging society. *Educational Gerontology, 25*(6), 581–593.

Kellough, R. D., & Kellough, N. G. (2003). *Teaching young adolescents: A guide to methods and resources* (4th ed.). Upper Saddle River, NJ: Merrill/Prentice Hall.

Kitwana, B. (2005). Why white kids love hip-hop: Wangstas, wiggers, wannabees, and the new reality of race in America. New York: Basic Civitas Books.

Krout, J. A., & Wasyliw, Z. (2002). Infusing gerontology into grades 7–12 social studies curricula. *Gerontologist, 42*(3), 387–391.

Kupetz, B. N. (1994). Ageism: A prejudice touching both young and old. *Day Care and Early Education, 21*, 34–37.

Langer, N. (1999). Changing youngsters' perceptions of aging: Aging education's role. *Educational Gerontology, 25*(6), 549–554.

Larue, G. A., & Seymour, R. (2005). Teaching respect: Giving children an understanding of their elders. Kingston, RI: Papier-Mache.

Manning, M. L. (2000, April). *Developmentally responsive multicultural education for young adolescents.* Paper presented at the Association for Childhood Education International, Baltimore, Maryland.

McGuire, S. L. (1993). Reduce ageism in kids by screening what they read. *Educational Digest, 59*(4), 63.

McGuire, S. L. (2003). Growing up and growing older: Books for young readers. *Childhood Education, 79*(3), 145–151.

Peacock, E. W., & Talley, W. M. (1984). Intergenerational contact: A way to counteract again. *Educational Gerontology, 10*(1–2), 13–24.

Population Reference Bureau (1999). *Aging in the United States: An education module.* Washington, DC.

Scott, T., Minichiello, V., & Browning, C. (1998). Secondary school students' knowledge of and attitudes toward older people. *Ageing & Society, 18*(2), 167.

Sheldon, J. P. (1998). Addressing stereotypes and ageism in a life span development course. *Teaching of Psychology, 25*(4), 291–293.

Sorgman, M. I., & Sorenson, M. (1984). Ageism: A course of study. *Theory into Practice, 23*(2), 117.

Stevenson, C. (2002). *Teaching ten to fourteen year olds* (3rd ed.). Boston: Allyn and Bacon.

Thornton, J. E. (2002). Myths of ageing or ageist stereotypes. *Educational Gerontology, 28*(4), 301–302.

Wircenski, M., Walker, M., Allen, J. & West, L. (1999). Age as a diversity issue in grades K–12 and in higher education. *Educational Gerontology, 25*(6), 491.

Internet Sites for Extending Thinking

Anxiety, Panic Disorder, Depression

http://www.adaa.org
Anxiety Disorders Association

http://www.nlm.nih.gov/medlineplus/nicdisorder.html
Federal government Medline Plus

http://www.bostoncoop.net/~tpryor/wiki/index.php?title=Ageism
Examples, responses, & links to further reading on ageism (from Wikpedia)

http://www.webster.edu/~woolflm/ageismlist.html
Includes theoretical basis, relationship of ageism to self-concept, gender and ageism, cross-cultural perspectives, and psychology and ageism (by L. Woolf, Webster University)

http://members.aol.com/lacillo/multicultural.html
Contains articles & links related to multicultural counseling

http://www.csriu.org
Offers strategies to help young people behave in a responsible, legal, and safe manner when using technology

http://www.wiredsafety.org
Provides information to internet and mobile device users of all ages, including to related sites, help with identity and credential theft, online fraud and cyberstalking, hacking, and malicious code attacks

Resource A

Creating Additional Context for a Given Case

It is important to bring your own knowledge and personal purpose to the analysis of a given case. Hence, the context of each case has not been highly prescribed. For example, the cases do not indicate grade level, thereby allowing for a variety of readers to bring their own grade-level context to the case.

Therefore, prior to analyzing a given case, you are invited to modify its context. Your instructor will help decide which cases might be modified and the extent of the modifications and will direct you to do so individually, in small groups, or as a class.

When so directed by your instructor, include factors that make the case richer, more authentic, or more personally meaningful to you, your small group, or your class. You may want to re-create a context that resembles a school in which you are currently completing a field experience or in which you are teaching, or you may want to create a setting representing the type of school that you hope to work in some day. Include one or two factors from the following categories.

Characteristics of the community. You might include such factors as proportion of socioeconomic, ethnic, and religious groups and the sociopolitical attitudes of various community groups.

Characteristics of the school. You might include demographics related to the ethnic, religious, and special needs makeup of the student body; curricular and extracurricular emphases of the school; and recent school reform efforts.

Nature of the characters and the classroom. You might include information such as personal characteristics (e.g., physical appearance, social abilities, mannerisms and behavioral habits, intellectual abilities, and teaching or learning styles) or grade level of the class, physical arrangement of the classroom, type of curriculum, and daily schedule of the classes.

In summary, prior to analyzing each case assigned by your instructor, take a few minutes to list two or three additional contextual variables that you believe are important.

Possible Cultural Contexts

Each of the cases will generate a richer and more meaningful discussion if set in an authentic educational and cultural context. To that end, several options are possible:

Scenario 1.   Decide that the school and classroom in which the case takes place are very diverse—with high proportions of students of color, lower socioeconomic status, disability, and the like greater than those of the general population. (See Table 1.1 and Table 1.2 for estimated populations of minority groups in the United States.)

Table 1.1 Estimated Population of Ethnic Groups in the United States, According to Race and Hispanic, Jewish, and Muslim Origins, 1990

Race	Percentage
All Persons	**100.0**
White Americans	80.3
African-Americans	12.1
American Indian, Eskimo, or Aleut	0.8
American Indians	0.8
Aleuts	0.0
Asian or Pacific Islander	2.9
Chinese Americans	0.7
Japanese Americans	0.3
Asian Indian	0.3
Korean Americans	0.3
Vietnamese	0.2
Native Hawaiians	0.1
Samoans	0.0
Guamanians	0.0
Other Asian or pacific Islander	0.3
Other	3.9
Hispanic Origin	
All persons	**100.00**
Hispanic Origin	9.0
Mexican	5.4
Puerto Rican	1.1
Cuban	0.4
Other Hispanic	2.0
Not of Hispanic Origin	91.0
Jewish and Muslim Origin	
All Persons	**100.0**
Jewish	2.8
Muslim	2.1

Source: Bennett, C. L. *Comprehensive Multicultural Education: Theory and Practice* (3rd ed.). Copyright (c)1995 by Allyn & Bacon. Reprinted/adapted by permission.

Table 1.2 Estimated Percentage of Children in Poverty; with Disabilities and of Gay/Lesbian/Bisexual Orientation

Poverty	*Percentage*
Children under the age of 18 who are poor (Reed & Sautter, 1990)	20
Exceptionality	
Children identified as having disabilities for purposes of special education services (U.S. Department of Education, 1994)	7.4
Sexual Orientation	
Persons of gay/lesbian/bisexual orientation (Kalota et al., 1994)	10

Scenario 2. Specify that the diversity in the community, school, and classroom in which the case takes place is equal to that of the general population.

Scenario 3. Specify that the diversity in the case school is equal to that of the school in which you are completing or have completed a field experience. It is recommended that this option be selected only when a specific and significant need suggests it. For example, if a school in which you work as a teacher's aide, a student teacher, or a teacher is 98 percent white and has recently experienced racial tension, you might decide to add such issues to a given case.

In addition to the types of diversity outlined in the tables, students in schools vary in other ways, including language, religious affiliation, and national creed. The reader is referred to other multicultural education sources for statistics on other groups and for additional data on the groups cited earlier.

Based on the percentages of various groups in the United States, as listed in Tables 1.1 and 1.2, the composition of a "typical" classroom of 30[*] students would be as shown in Table 1.3.

Obviously, such a "typical" class rarely exists. It is constructed here for those who would want to set the cases provided in a classroom representing the diversity of persons in the general population. Because the student bodies in many schools consist of much greater proportions of ethnic diversity than does the general population, when analyzing a given case you should assume that the story takes place in such a school. Doing so will better prepare you for a career that might well include teaching in a school with a rich diversity of students.

Once you have predetermined the ethnic, socioeconomic, religious, exceptionality, and sexual orientation of the students in a case, establish other classroom, school, and community

---

[*]Because a given student may well belong to more than one group, the total number of students listed exceeds 30.

Table 1.3 Composition of a Classroom of 30 students*

Students	Number
White	20
African-American	4
Asian	1
American Indian	1
Hispanic	3
Jewish	1
Muslim	1
Poor	6
With disabilities	2–3
Gay/lesbian/bisexual	3

*Based on estimated population of ethnic, socioeconomic class, poverty, exceptionality, and sexual orientation.

characteristics that will further provide the context for the case. For example, specify factors such as the following:

- Number of students served in the school
- Number of students in the particular classroom
- School budget
- Performance levels of students on statewide achievement tests

Furthermore, specify the following:

- Whether the school tracks students into several levels
- Whether the school has access to tutors and student teachers in a teacher education program in a local college
- Whether the school has class periods of a certain length (e.g., 50, 60, or 90 minutes)
- Whether the school has stand-alone and online access to sophisticated computer and related technologies
- Whether the school has a well-developed parent-involvement program

Examples of contexts that might be designed as a basis for the analysis of a given case follow.

Example I. Longfellow School serves 1,000 low- and low-middle-income students living in the inner city. Typical classroom size is 25 students. The student body is 40 percent African-American, 10 percent Hispanic-American, 5 percent Asian-American, 5 percent Native American, and 40 percent White. Approximately 20 percent of these students are Jewish. Student scores on standardized achievement tests are in the 70th percentile. The school divides students into three tracks. Thirty-nine percent of graduates go on to college. Reform efforts have moved the school to the fore in terms of offering a well-developed multicultural curriculum.

Example II. Lincoln School in a city of 40,000 serves 500 low-SES pupils. The student body is 70 percent White, 20 percent Native American, and 10 percent African-American.

Approximately 40 percent of the students come from farms. Fifty percent of pupils come from single-parent families, and half are from families that claim to be devoutly Catholic. Class size in Lincoln is 30 students per room. Each room has two computers with Internet interface, and two computer labs of 20 computers each are available to teachers. Except for the progressive approach to technology, the curriculum is relatively traditional. Parent involvement in school activities is low.

Each of these examples emphasizes different characteristics in terms of ethnicity, SES, religion, family structure, curriculum, and the like. Each could have been more or less elaborate, depending on the nature of the case to be analyzed, the needs and interests of the students analyzing the case, and the goals of the course or workshop within which the case is used.

Resource B

Banks's Approaches for the Integration of Multicultural Content

Approach	Description	Examples	Strengths	Problems
Contributions	Heroes, cultural components, holidays, and other discrete elements related to ethnic groups are added to the curriculum on special days, occasions, and celebrations.	Famous Mexican-Americans are studied only during the week of Cinco de Mayo (May 5) . African-Americans are studied during African-American History Month in February but rarely during the rest of the year. Ethnic foods are studied in the first grade with little attention devoted to the cultures in which the foods are embedded.	Provides a quick and relatively easy way to put ethnic content into the curriculum. Gives ethnic heroes visibility in the curriculum alongside main stream heroes. Is a popular approach among teachers and educators.	Results in a superficial understanding of ethnic cultures. Focuses on the lifestyles and artifacts of ethnic groups and reinforces stereotypes and misconceptions. Mainstream criteria are used to select heroes and cultural elements for inclusion in the curriculum.
Additive	This approach consists of the addition of content, concept, themes, and perspectives to the curriculum without changing its structures.	Adding the book *The Color Purple* to a literature unit without reconceptualizing the unity or giving the students the background knowledge to understand the book. Adding a unit on the Japanese-American internment to a U.S. history course without treating the Japanese in any other unit. Leaving the core curriculum intact but adding an ethnic studies course as an elective that focuses on a specific ethnic group.	Makes it possible to add ethnic content to the curriculum without changing its structure, which requires substantial curriculum changes and staff development. Can be implemented within the existing curriculum structure.	Reinforces the idea that ethnic history and culture are not integral parts of U.S. mainstream culture. Students view ethnic groups from Anglocentric and Eurocentric perspectives. Fails to help students understand how the dominant culture and ethnic cultures are interconnected and interrelated.

Note: Banks, J.A. (2005). *Multicultural education: Issues and perspectives* (5th ed.). New York: Wiley. Reprinted with permission of John Wiley & Sons, Inc.

Approach	Description	Examples	Strengths	Problems
Transformation	The basic goals, structure, and nature of the curriculm are changed to enable students to view concepts, events, issues, problems, and themes from the perspectives of diverse cultural, ethnic, and racial groups.	A unit on the American Revolution describes the meaning of the revolution to Anglo revolutionaries, Anglo loyalists, African-Americans, Indians, and the British. A unit on 20th-century U.S. literature includes works by William Faulkner, Joyce Carol Oates, Langston Hughes, N. Scott Momaday, Saul Bellow, Maxine Hong Kingston, Rudolfo A. Anaya, and Piri Thomas.	Enables students to understand the complex ways in which diverse racial and cultural groups participated in the formation of U.S. society and culture. Helps reduce racial and ethnic encapsulation. Enables diverse ethnic, racial, and religious groups to see their cultures' ethos and perspectives in the school curriculum. Gives students a balanced view of the nature and development of U.S. culture and society. Helps to empower victimized racial, ethnic, and cultural groups.	The implementation of this approach requires substantial curriculum revision, in-service training, and the identification and development of materials written from the perspectives of various racial and cultural groups. Staff development for the institutionalization of this approach must be continual and ongoing.
Social Action	In this approach, students identify important social problems and issues, gather pertinent data, clarify their values on the issues, make decisions, and take reflective actions to help resolve the issue or problem.	A class studies prejudice and discrimination in its school and decides to take actions to improve race relations in the school. A class studies the treatment of ethnic groups in a local newspaper and writes a letter to the publisher suggesting ways that the treatment of ethnic groups in the newspaper should be improved.	Enables students to improve their thinking, value school and analysis, decision-making and social-action skills. Enables students to improve their data gathering skills. Helps students develop a sense of political efficacy. Helps students improve their skills to work in groups.	Requires a considerable amount of curriculum planning and materials identification. May be longer in duration than more traditional teaching units. May focus on problems and issues considered controversial by some members of the school staff and citizens of the community. Students may be able to take few meaningful actions that contribute to the resolution of the social issue or problem.

Resource C

Design Your Own Case

Author Name(s): _____

Title of Case: _____ **Grade Level(s):** _____

Subject Matter Area (e.g., science): _____

Generic Teaching Topic (e.g., planning, grading): _____

Contextual Information:

_____

Community Factors:

_____

School Factors:

_____

Classroom Factors:

_____

Teacher Characteristics:

_____

Student Characteristics:

_____

Characteristics of Curriculum:

_____

_____

Story: _____

_____

_____

_____

_____

_____

Questions for Reflection:

1. _____
   _____

2. _____
   _____

3. _____
   _____

Activities for Extending Thinking:

1. _____
   _____

2. _____
   _____

Criteria for assessing responses to your Questions for Reflection:

List criteria (e.g., response is clear, consistent with research or best practice, generalized to an appropriate degree—not overgeneralized, valid—based on facts in the case, relevant to an issue in the case, other).

1. _____
   _____

2. _____
   _____

Responses to Questions for Reflection:

List what you would consider to be examples of acceptable and unacceptable responses.

	Acceptable	Unacceptable
1. a.	_____	_____
b.	_____	_____
2. a.	_____	_____
b.	_____	_____

Responses to Activities for Extending Thinking:

List examples of acceptable and unacceptable responses.

1.	_____	_____
2.	_____	_____

Resource D

Matrix: Interpersonal Competence Cases, Multicultural Content Cases

The following is a taxonomy that places each of the cases in the casebook into one or both of the following areas:

- **Interpersonal Competence.** Ability to interpret intentional communications (language, signs, gestures), unconscious cues (body language), and customs in cultural styles different from one's own. Emphasis is on empathy and interpersonal communication (Bennett, C., *Multicultural Education,* 1999, p. 30). Relates to interaction with students.
- **Multicultural Content.** Knowledge of history, heritage, and culture of persons of cultures different from one's own. Relates to subject matter (curriculum) planned for or delivered to students.

	Interpersonal Competence	Multicultural Content
Chapter 2 Gender		
Case 1 Reinforcing Specifically	X	
Case 2 Fridays Are Video Days	X	
Case 3 Developing Skills of Critical Analysis: Exposing the Myths of Films and Fairy Tales		X
Case 4 Dwight, What Do You Think?	X	
Case 5 integrating Women's Issues into Curriculum		X
Chapter 3 Ethnicity		
Case 6 Let's All Make Up the Rules for Our Classroom	X	
Case 7 Other Cultures Celebrate Thanksgiving, Too		X
Case 8 When Will I Ever Use This? Mathematics and Social Justice		X
Case 9 Overlook the Stereotypes—It's Art		X
Case 10 Presidents of Mount Rushmore: Another Perspective		X
Chapter 4 Race		
Case 11 The Knowledge Base on Diversity: An Aid for Teachers		X
Case 12 Students Right an Injustice	X	X

	Interpersonal Competence	Multicultural Content
Case 13 Use of the N-Word in the Classroom	X	
Case 14 Hey, Teach—You Trippin' on Me, but Not on the White Kids!	X	
Case 15 A Lesson on Oppression and Whiteness		X
Chapter 5 Socioeconomic Status		
Case 16 A New Student and a Lesson in Geography	X	
Case 17 Gangs and the Victims of Violence—Writing as a Therapy	X	
Case 18 How Should I Grade Danielle?	X	
Case 19 Rewarding Respectful Behavior	X	
Chapter 6 Religion		
Case 20 Isn't the Christmas Tree a Christian Symbol?	X	X
Case 21 My Persuasive Essay Is "Why We Should Follow Jesus"	X	X
Case 22 Planning for Religious Diversity: Special Needs of Muslim Students	X	X
Chapter 7 Special Needs		
Case 23 We Only Meant It as a Joke	X	
Case 24 Structuring for Success in a Mainstreamed Classroom	X	
Case 25 Anthony, Please Don't Push: Designing an IEP	X	
Case 26 Inaccessibility of Web Sites to Students Who Are Blind	X	
Chapter 8 Sexual Orientation		
Case 27 Not in My Group—He's Gay!	X	
Case 28 In Islam, Homosexuality Is a Sin and a Crime	X	X
Case 29 "Lesbian": Responding to Name-Calling	X	
Chapter 9 Language		
Case 30 You'll Need Both Black Vernacular and Standard English	X	X
Case 31 They Speak English and Spanish Well, but a Learning Disability Creates Problems in Reading and Writing	X	
Case 32 A Bilingual Teacher's Aide Assesses His New School	X	X
Case 33 Computers and Culturally Diverse Learners	X	
Chapter 10 Ageism		
Case 34 Age as a Factor in Bullying and "Cyberbullying"	X	

Resource E

Bibliography of Multicultural Children's Literature

Part I: Print Resources

African

Archibald, E. F. (1997). *A Sudanese family*. Minneapolis, MN: Lerner.
Berg, L. E. (1997). *An Eritrean family*. Minneapolis, MN: Lerner.
Bryan, N. (2004). *Somali Americans*. Edina, MN: Abdo Publishing.
Chicoine, S. (1997). *A Liberian famliy*. Minneapolis, MN: Lerner.
Dee, R. (1988). *Two ways to count to ten: A Liberian folk tale*. New York: Holt.
Hoffman, M. (2002). *The color of home*. New York: Phyllis Fogelman.
Kurtz, J. (1998). *The storyteller's beads*. Orlando, FL: Harcourt.

Asian American

Hmong

A free people: Our stories, our voices, our dreams. (1994). Minneapolis: The Project.
Brown, J. (2004). *Little cricket*. Albany, NY: Book House of Stuyvesant Plaza.
Cha, D. (2002). *Dia's story cloth*. St. Paul, MN: Minnesota Humanities Commission.
Murphy, N. (1997). *A Hmong family*. Minneapolis, MN: Lerner.
Shea, P. D. (1995). *The whispering cloth*. Illustrated by Anita Riggio. Stitched by You Yang. Boyds Mills, Pennsylvania: Boyds Mills Press.

Cambodian

Lipp, F. (2001). *The caged birds of Phnom penh*. Illustrated by Ronald Himler. New York: Holiday House.

Chinese

Cheng, A. (2000). *Grandfather counts*. New York: Lee & Low.
Chinn, K. (1995). *Sam and the lucky money*. New York: Lee & Low.
Demi. (1990). *The empty pot*. New York: Henry Holt.

Lee, M. (2001). *Earthquake*. Illustrated by Yangsook Choi. New York: Frances Foster.

Lewis, R. (2000). *I love you like crazy cakes*. Illustrated by Jane Dyer. New York: Little, Brown.

Roth, S. L. (2001). *Happy birthday Mr. Kang*. Washington, DC: National Geographic Society.

Wong, J. S. (1994). *Good luck gold and other poems*. New York: Margaret K. McElderry.

Wong, J. S. (1996). *A suitcase of seaweed and other poems*. New York: Margaret K. McElderry.

Wong, J. S. (2000). *The trip back home*. Illustrated by Bo Jia. New York: Harcourt.

Wong, J. S. (2000). *This next New Year*. Illustrated by Yangsook Choi. New York: Frances Foster.

Wong, J. S. (2002). *Apple pie 4th of July*. Illustrated by Margaret Chodes-Irvine. New York: Harcourt.

Japanese

Bunting, E. (1998). *So far from the sea*. Illustrated by Chris K. Soentpiet. New York: Scholastic.

Mochizuki, K. (1993). *Baseball saved us*. Illustrated by Dom Lee. New York: Lee & Low.

Say, A. (1993). *Grandfather's journey*. Boston: Houghton Mifflin.

Uchida, Y. (1993). *The bracelet*. Illustrated by Joanna Yardley. New York: Philomel.

Korean

Balgassi, H. (1996). *Peacebound trains*. Boston: Clarion.

Balgassi, H. (1997). *Tae's sonata*. Boston: Clarion.

Choi, Y. (2001). *The name jar*. New York: Knopf.

Pak, S. (1999). *Dear Juno*. Illustrated by Susan Kathleen Hartung. New York: Viking.

Pak, S. (2002). *A place to grow*. Illustrated by Marcelino Truong. New York: Arthur A. Levine.

Park, F. & Park, G. (1998). *My freedom trip: A child's escape from North Korea*. Illustrated by Debra Reid Jenkins.Washington, DC: National Geographic.

Park, F. & Park, G. (2002). *Good-bye, 382 Shin Dang Dong*. Washington, DC: National Geographic.

Recorvits, H. (2003). *My name is Yoon*. Illustrated by Gabi Swiatkowska. New York: Frances Foster.

Philippino

Gilles, A. A. (2001). *Willie wins*. New York: Lee & Low.

Thai

Ho, M. (1996). *Hush: A Thai lullaby*. Illustrated by Holly Meade. New York: Orchard.

Tibetan

Dolphin, L. (1997). *Our journey from Tibet*. New York: Dutton Children's Books.
Perry, A. (1999). *The Tibetans*. New York: Viking Studio.

Vietnamese

Breckler, R. (1996). *Sweet dried apples: A Vietnamese wartime childhood*. Boston: Houghton Mifflin.
Garland, S. (1993). *The Lotus seed*. Illustrated by Tatsuro Kiuchi. New York: Harcourt Brace.
McKay, L., Jr. (1998). *Journey home*. New York: Lee & Low.
O'Connor, K. (1992). *Dan Thuy's new life in America*. Minneapolis, MN: Lerner.
Shea, P. D. (2003). *Ten mice for tet*. San Francisco: Chronicle Books.

Afghani

Kazem, H. (2003). *Afghanistan*. Gareth Stevens.
Khan, R. (1998). *King of the skies*. Toronto: Stoddart Kids.
Khan, R. (1998). *The roses in my carpets*. Toronto: Stoddart Kids.
Khan, R. (2003). *Ruler of the courtyard*. East Rutherford, NJ: Viking Children's Books.

Bosnian

Landew Silverman, R. (1997). *A Bosnian family*. Minneapolis, MN: Lerner.

Indian

Krishnaswami, U. (2003). *Monsoon*. New York: Farrar, Straus, Giroux.

Islam/Muslim

Demi, (2003). *Muhammad*. New York: Simon & Schuster.
Khan, R. (1998). *Muslim child*. Toronto: Napoleon.
Macaulay, D. (2003). *Mosque*. Boston: Houghton Mifflin.
Stanley, D. (2002). *Saladin: Noble prince of Islam*. New York: HarperCollins.

Jewish American

Adelman, P. (1998). *The Bible from alef to tav*. Los Angeles: Tora Aura.
Battermamn, L. C. (1997). *Two cents and a milk bottle*. Los Angeles: Tora Aura.
Bierman, C. (1998). *Journey to Ellis Island*. New York: Hyperion.
Blos, J. (1994). *Brooklyn doesn't rhyme*. New York: Atheneum.
Hurwitz, J. (1992). *Once I was a plum tree*. Beech Tree.
Kimmelman, L. (2000). *Dance, sing, remember: A celebration of Jewish holidays*. New York: HarperCollins.
Lasky, K. (1998). *Dreams in the golden country: The diary of Zipporah Felman, a Jewish immigrant girl*. New York: Scholastic.

Palestinian

Clinton, C. (2002). *A stone in my hand.* Cambridge, MA: Candlewick.

Nye, N. (1997). *Sitti's secret.* New York: Four Winds.

Latino

Ada, A. F. (1997). *Gathering the sun: An alphabet in Spanish and English.* Illustrated by Simon Silva. New York: HarperCollins.

Ada, A. F. (2002). *I love Saturdays y domingos.* Illustrated by Elivia Savadier. New York: Atheneum Books for Young Readers.

Altman, L. J. (1993). *Amelia's road.* Illustrated by Enrique O. Sanchez. New York: Lee & Low.

Anzaldua, G. (1993). *Friends from the other side: Amigos delotro lado.* Illustrated by Consuelo Mendez. San Francisco: Children's Book Press.

Cool salsa: Bilingual poems on growing up Latino in the United States. (1994). New York: Fawcett Juniper.

Delacre, L. (1993). *Vejigante masquerader.* New York: Scholastic.

Dorros, A. (1991). *Abuela.* Illustrated by Elisa Kleven. New York: Puffin.

Dorros, A. (1995). *Isla.* Illustrated by Elisa Kleven. New York: Dutton Children's Books.

Fine, B. H. (1999). *Under the lemon moon.* Illustrated by Rene King Moreno. New York: Lee & Low.

Garza, C. L. (1996). *In my family: En mi familia.* San Francisco: Children's Book Press.

Grossman, P. (1994). *Saturday market.* Illustrated by Enrique O. Sanchez. New York: Lothrop, Lee & Shepard.

Jimenez, F. (1998). *La mariposa.* Illustrated by Simon Silva. Boston: Houghton Mifflin.

Johnston, T. (2001). *Uncle rain cloud.* Illustrated by Fabricio VandenBroeck. Watertown, MA: Charlesbridge.

Katz, K. (1999). *The colors of us.* New York: Holt.

Krull, K. (2003). *Harvesting hope: The story of Cesar Chavez.* Illustrated by Yuyi Morales. New York: Harcourt.

Mora, P. (1996). *Confetti: Poems for children.* Illustrated by Enrique O. Sanchez. New York: Lee & Low.

Mora, P. (1997). *Tomas and the library lady.* Illustrated by Raul Colón. New York: Knopf.

Mora, P. (1999). *The rainbow tulip.* Illustrated by Elizabeth Sayles. New York: Viking.

Mora, P. (2001). *Love to mama: A tribute to mothers.* Illustrated by Paula S. Barragan. New York: Lee & Low.

Perez, L. K. (2002). *First day in grapes.* Illustrated by Robert Casilla. New York: Lee & Low.

Rosa-Casanova, S. (1997). *Mama provi and the pot of rice.* Illustrated by Robert Roth. New York: Aladdin Paperbacks.

Soto, G. (1993). *Too many tamales.* Illustrated by Ed Martinez. New York: Putnam.

Soto, G. (2002). *If the shoe fits.* Illustrated by Terry Widener. New York: Putnam.

Wolf, B. (1994). *Beneath the stone: A Mexican Zapotec tale.* New York: Orchard.

Native American

Bruchac, J. & London, J. (1992). *Thirteen moons on turtle's back.* Illustrated by Thomas Locker. New York: Philomel.

Bruchac, J. (1993). *The first strawberries: A cherokee story.* Illustrated by Anna Vojtech. New York: Dial Books for Young Readers.

Bruchac, J. (1994). *A boy called slow.* Illustrated by Rocco Baviera. New York: Philomel.

Bruchac, J. (1996). *The circle of thanks: Native American poems and songs of thanksgiving.* Illustrated by Murv Jacob. Mahwah, NJ: Bridgewater.

Bruchac, J. (1997). *Many nations: An alphabet of Native America.* Illustrated by Robert F. Goetzl. Mahwah, NJ: BridgeWater.

Goble, P. (1999). *Paul Goble gallery: Three Native American stories.* New York: Simon & Schuster Books for Young Readers.

Grossman, V. (1991). *Ten little rabbits.* Illustrated by Sylvia Long. San Francisco: Chronicle.

Highway, T. (2001). *Caribou song.* Illustrated by Brian Deines. Toronto: HarperCollins.

Hobbs, W. (1997). *Beardream.* Illustrated by Jill Kastner. New York: Aladdin Paperbacks.

Leitich Smith, C. (2000). *Jingle dancer.* Illustrated by Cornelius Van Wright and Ying-Hwa Hu. New York: Morrow Junior Books.

Littlechild, G. (1993). *This land is my land.* San Francisco: Children's Book Press.

Martin, R. (1992). *The rough-face girl.* Illustrated by David Shannon. New York: Putnam.

Mitchell, B. (1996). *Red bird.* Illustrated by Todd L. W. Doney. New York: Lothrop, Lee & Shepard.

McLerran, A. (1995). *The ghost dance.* Paintings by Paul Morin. New York: Clarion.

Ortiz, S. J. (2001). *The people shall continue.* San Francisco: Children's Book Press.

Osofsky, A. (1992). *Dreamcatcher.* Illustrated by Ed Young. New York: Orchard.

Oughton, J. (1992). *How the stars fell into the sky: A Navajo legend.* Boston: Houghton Mifflin.

Swann, G. (1998). *Touching the distance: Native American riddle-poems.* Illustrated by Maria Rendon. New York: Browndeer.

Waboose, J. B. (2000). *Sky sisters.* Illustrated by Brian Deines. Toronto: Kids Can.

African American

Bradby, M. (1995). *More than anything else.* Illustrated by Chris K. Soentpiet. New York: Orchard.

Bridges, R. (1999). *Through my eyes.* New York: Scholastic.

Bryan, A. (1997). *Ashley Bryan's ABC of African American poetry.* New York: Atheneum Books for Young Readers.

Collier, B. (2000). *Uptown.* New York: Henry Holt.

Fitzgerald Howard, E. (2000). *Virgie goes to school with us boys.* Illustrated by E. B. Lewis. New York: Simon & Schuster Books for Young Readers.

Hoffman, M. (1991). *Amazing grace*. Illustrated by Caroline Binch. New York: Dial Books for Young Readers.

Hudson, W. (1993). *Pass it on: African-American poetry for children*. Illustrated by Floyd Cooper. New York: Scholastic.

Johnson, D. (2000). *Quinnie blue*. Illustrated by James Ransome. New York: Henry Holt.

King Farris, C. (2003). *My brother Martin: A sister remembers growing up with the Rev. Dr. Martin Luther King Jr.* Illustrated by Chris Soentpiet. New York: Simon & Schuster Books for Young Readers.

King Mitchell, M. (1993). *Uncle Jed's barbershop*. Illustrated by James Ransome. New York: Simon & Schuster Books for Young Readers.

Littlesugar, A. (1999). *Tree of hope*. Illustrated by Floyd Cooper. New York: Philomel.

Littlesugar, A. (2001). *Freedom school, yes!* Illustrated by Floyd Cooper. New York: Philomel.

Monk, I. (1999). *Hope*. Illustrated by Janice Lee Porter. Minneapolis: Carolrhoda.

Munoz Ryan, P. (2002). *When Marion sang*. Illustrated by Brian Selznick. New York: Scholastic.

Perdomo, W. (2002). *Visiting Langston*. Illustrated by Bryan Collier. New York: Holt.

Ringgold, F. (1991). *Tar beach*. New York: Crown.

Steptoe, J. (1987). *Mufaro's beautiful daughters*. New York: Lothrop, Lee & Shepard.

Taulbert, C. L. (2001). *Little Cliff's first day of school*. Illustrated by E. B. Lewis. New York: Dial Books for Young Readers.

Taylor, M. D. (1987). *The friendship*. Illustrated by Max Ginsburg. New York: Dial Books for Readers.

Williams, S. A. (1992). *Working cotton*. Illustrated by Carole Byard. New York: Harcourt Brace Jovanovich.

Woodson, J. (2001). *The other side*. Illustrated by E. B. Lewis. New York: Putnam.

Woodson, J. (2002). *Visiting day*. Illustrated by James E. Ransome. New York: Scholastic.

Words with wings: A treasury of African-American poetry and art. (2000). New York: Harper.

Multiracial

Igus, T. (1997). *Two Mrs. Gibsons*. Berkeley, CA: Children's Book Press.

Wing, N. (1996). *Jalapeno bagels*. New York: Antheneum.

Race Relations

McKee, D. (1979). *Tusk tusk*. La Jolla, CA: Kane/Miller.

Scholes, K. (1989). *Peace begins with you*. New York: Little, Brown Children's.

Vaugelade, A. (2001). *The War*. Minneapolis, MN: Carolrhoda.

Wood, D. (1991). *Old turtle*. Duluth, MN: Pfeifer-Hamilton.

Chapter Books

Ada, A. F. (1993). *My name is Maria Isabel*. New York: Aladdin Paperbacks.

American eyes: New Asian-American short stories for young adults. (1994). New York: Holt.

Atkin, S. B. (1993). *Voices from the fields: Children of migrant farm workers tell their stories*. New York: Little, Brown.

Bruchac, J. (1997). *Eagle song*. New York: Puffin

Clinton, C. (2002). *A stone in my hand*. Cambridge, MA: Candlewick.

Curtis, C. P. (1995). *The Watsons go to Birmingham—1963*. New York: Bantam Doubleday Bell Books for Young Readers.

Curtis, C. P. (1999). *Bud, not buddy*. New York: Delacorte.

Danticat, E. (2002). *Behind the mountains*. New York: Orchard.

Dorris, M. (1992). *Morning girl*. New York: Scholastic.

Dorris, M. (1994). *Guests*. New York: Scholastic.

Erdrich, L. (1999). *The birchbark house*. New York: Hyperion Books for Children.

Flake, S. G. (1998). *The skin I'm in*. New York: Hyperion Books for Children.

Forester, S. (1999) *Dust from old bones*. New York: Morrow/Harper.

Hamilton, V. (1993). *Many thousand gone: African Americans from slavery to freedom*. Illustrated by Leo and Diane Dillon. New York: Knopf.

Hesse, K. (1992). *Letters from Rifka*. New York: Holt.

Ho, M. (1991). *The clay marble*. New York: Farrar Straus Giroux.

Jimenez, F. (2001). *Breaking through*. Boston: Houghton Mifflin.

Leitich Smith, C. (2001). *Rain is not my Indian name*. New York: HarperCollins.

Lowry, L. (1989). *Number the stars*. New York: Bantam Doubleday Bell Books for Young Readers.

Mohr, N. (1979). *Felita*. New York: Puffin.

Mohr, N. (1986). *Going home*. New York: Puffin.

Munoz Ryan, P. (2000). *Esperanza rising*. New York: Scholastic.

Na, A. (2001). *A step from heaven*. New York: Front Street.

Naidoo, B. (1986). *Journey to Jo'burg: A South African story*. New York: Harper Row.

Naidoo, B. (2000). *The other side of truth*. New York: Amistad.

Naidoo, B. (2003). *Out of bounds: Seven stories of conflict and hope*. New York: HarperCollins.

Namioka, L. (1992). *Yang the youngest and his terrible ear*. New York: Bantam Doubleday Bell Books for Young Readers.

Nye, N. (1997). *Habibi*. New York: Simon & Schuster.

Reilly Giff, P. (1997). *Lily's crossing*. New York: Dell Yearling.

Soto, G. (1990). *Baseball in April and other stories*. New York: Harcourt Brace.

Soto, G. (1992). *The skirt*. New York: Dell Publishing.

Taylor, M. D. (1976). *Roll of thunder, hear my cry*. New York: Puffin.

Taylor, M. D. (1981). *Let the circle be unbroken*. New York: Puffin.

Taylor, M. D. (1989). *The friendship and the gold Cadillac*. New York: Bantam Skylark.

Taylor, M. D. (1990). *Mississippi bridge*. New York: Skylark.

Taylor, M. D. (1990). *The road to Memphis*. New York: Puffin.

Taylor, M. D. (1995) . *The well*. New York: Scholastic.

Taylor, M. D. (2001). *The land*. New York: Phyllis Fogelman.

Uchida, Y. (1978). *Journey home*. New York: Aladdin Paperbacks.

Uchida, Y. (1981). *A jar of dreams*. New York: Aladdin Paperbacks.

Veciana-Suarez, A. (2002). *Flight to freedom*. New York: Orchard.

Yep, L. (1989). *The cook's family*. New York: Penguin Putnam.

Yep, L. (1991). *The star fisher*. New York: Puffin.

Yep, L. (2000). *Cockroach cooties*. New York: Hyperion Paperbacks for Children.

Reviews, Guides, Curricular References on Multicultural Children's Literature

Birdseye, D. T. (1997). *Under our skin: Kids talk about race*. New York: Holiday House.

Blakemore, C. (2002). *Faraway places: Your source for picture books that fly children to 82 countries*. Albany, WI: Adams-Pomroy.

Galda, L., & Cullinan, B. E. (2002). *Literature and the child* (5th ed.). Belmont, CA: Wadsworth/Thomson Learning.

Gangi, J. M. (2004). *Encountering children's literature: An arts approach*. New York: Pearson.

Harris, V. J. (1997). *Using multiethnic literature in the K–8 classroom*. Massachusetts: Christopher-Gordon.

Helbig, A. (2001). *Many peoples, one land: A guide to new multicultural literature for children and young adults*. Westport, CT: Greenwood.

Kruse, G.M., & Horning, K.T. (1991–1996). *Multicultural literature for children and young adults (Vol. 2)*. Madison, WI: Cooperative Children's Book Center of the University of Wisconsin—Madison.

Mitchell, D. (2003). *Children's literature: An invitation to the world*. Boston: Allyn and Bacon.

New press guide to multicultural resources for young readers. (1997). New York: Norton.

Nodelman, P., & Reimer, M. (2003). *The pleasures of children's literature*. New York: Allyn and Bacon.

Open the books and see all the people. (2000). Jamaica, NY: Queens Borough Public Library.

Opitz, M. F. (1998). *Literacy instruction for culturally and linguistically diverse students*. Newark, DE: International Reading Association.

Risko, V. J., & Bromley, K. (2001). *Collaboration for diverse learners: Viewpoints and practices*. Newark, DE: International Reading Association.

Schon, I. (2000). *Recommended books in Spanish for children and young adults 1996–1999*. Lanham, MD: Scarecrow.

Smith, D. J. (2002). *If the world were a village: A book about the world's people*. New York: Philomel.

Part II: Internet Resources
Children's Literature—General

Carol Hurst's Children's Literature Site http://www.carolhurst.com
Children's Literature Web Guide http://www.acs.ucalgary.ca/~dkbrown/index.html
Kathy Schrock's Guide for Educators: Literature and Language Arts
    http://www.school.discovery.com/schrockguide/arts/artlit.html
Kay E. Vandergrift's Special Interest Page
    http://www.scils.rutgers.edu/special/kay/kayhp2.html
Book Links http://www.ala.org/BookLinks
Horn Book http://www.hbook.com
Caldecott Medal Home Page http://www.ala.org:80/ala/alsc/caldecott.html
John Newberry Medal Home Page http://www.ala.org:80/alac/newberry.html
Coretta Scott King Award http://www.ala.org:80/srrt/index.html
The Americas Award http://www.uwm.edu/Dept/CLACS/outreachamericas.html
The Pura Belpore Award http://www.ala.org:80/ala/alsc/belpre.html
Michael L. Printz Award www.ala.org/yalsa/printz

Advocacy and Educational Equity

Children's Defense Fund www.childrensdefense.org/
Diversity University, Inc. www.du.org/
Equity Assistance Centers www.ed.gov/about/contacts/gen/othersites/equity.html
National Coalition of Advocates for Students www.ncas1.org
South Central Equity Assistance Center www.idra.org/scce/
Women and Minorities in Science and Engineering www.mills.edu

African-American

Black History Activities www.kn.pacbell.com/wired/BHM/AfroAm.html
Black History Treasure Hunt and Quiz www.kn.pacbell.com/wired/BHM/bhhuntquiz.html
Juneteenth www.juneteenth.com
African Art—Aesthetics and Meaning http://www.lib.virginia.edu/clemons/RMC/exhib/
    93.ray.aa/African.html

Asian-American

AskAsia Homepage www.askasia.org
China the Beautiful, Chinese Art and Literature www.chinapage.com/china.html
Japanese American National Museum www.janm.org/main.htm
Joseph Wu's Origami Page www.origami.vancouver.bc.ca

Lo Latino

Artes e Historia de Mexico www.arts-history.mx/direc.html
Azteca Web Page www.azteca.net/aztec
Centro Virtual Cervantes www.cvc.cervantes.es/portada.htm
Cinco de Mayo latino.sscnet.ucla.edu/demo/cinco.html
Cinco de Mayo Webquest www.zianet.com/cjcox/edutech4learning/cinco.html
Hispanic Contributions to History www.neta.com/~1stbooks/content.htm
Hispanic Magazine www.hisp.com
Hispanic Reading Room, Library of Congress lcweb.loc.gov/rr/hispanic
Indigenous Mexican Images www.azteca.net/aztec/prehisp/index.shtml
Latin American Network Information Center lanic.utexas.edu
Mexico para Ninos www.elbalero.gob.mx
Mundo Latino www.mundolatino.org/cultura
Mundo Maya www.mexicodesconocido.com.mx/indigena/mundmaya.htm
National Council of La Raza www.nclr.org
National Latino Communications Center www.nlcc.com/
Nuestro México www.mexico.udg.mx
Oaxacan Pottery www.manos.de.oaxaca.com
Society for the Advancement of Chicanos and Native Americans in Science
    www.sacnas.org

Multicultural Education

Amigos edweb.sdsu.edu/people/cguanipa/amigos
Institute for Global Communications www.igc.org/igc
Multicultural Book Review www.isomedia.com/homes/jmele/homepage.html
Teaching to Change the World—Jeannie Oakes
    www.mhhe.com/socscience/education/oakes
Virtual Library on Migration & Ethnic Relations www.ercomer.org/wwwvl

Native Americans

American Indian Heritage Foundation www.indians.org/AboutUs/aboutus.html
Anasazi Great Kiva 3D Tour sipapu.ucsb.edu/html/kiva.html
Bureau of Indians Affairs www.doi.gov/bureau-indian-affairs.html
National Museum of the American Indian www.si.edu/nmai
Native American Indian Resources www.kstrom.net/isk/mainmenu.html
Native American Stories: Books and E-texts www.kstrom.net/isk/stories/ebooks.html
NativeWeb—an Internet Community www.nativeweb.org
Society for the Advancement of Chicanos and Native Americans in Science
    www.sacnas.org
WWW Virtual Library: American Indians www.hanksville.org/NAresources/

Women and Girls

Bilingual Women of NASA quest.arc.nasa.gov/women/espanol/intro.html
Computer Research Association: Women www.cra.org/Activities/craw
Exploring Your Future in Math and Science www.cs.wisc.edu/~karavan/afl/home.html
Girl Games Inc www.girlgamesinc.com
Girl Tech www.girltech.com/index.html
GrayMill—Gender Equity www.graymill.com
National Women's History Project www.nwhp.org
New Moon Publishing www.newmoon.org/
Tapping Interest Resources for Women in Computer Science tap.mills.edu/
University of Wisconsin Women and Science Programs www.uwosh.edu/programs/wis
Women of NASA quest.arc.nasa.gov/women/intro.html

Resource F

Sample Rubrics for Assessing Student Responses to Cases

The following two rubrics for assessing student responses to cases have proven to be useful. The first, entitled "Rubric for Assessment of Case Analysis Process," provides a format for student self-assessment, peer assessment, and instructor assessment of the process aspects of case analysis, i.e., the level of participation of each student. When working in small groups, students seem to especially appreciate the opportunity to assess peer contributions, i.e., to be able to reward active participation and hold accountable those who might tend to be less participatory. This form may be used regularly after each and every small group case analysis, or periodically; its impending use may be announced at the beginning of the term and/or on each day it is to be used.

The second rubric, entitled "Rubric for Instructor Rating of Case Analysis Products" has been helpful in delineating criteria for assessing the products submitted by individuals or groups of students. As with any rubric, criteria may be altered for any given case analysis. For example, if the "Questions for Reflection" ask students to relate a given case to lesson planning, then the criteria (bottom left-hand side of the rubric) that asks students to relate the issues in the case to up to six factors, might be adjusted by the instructor to focus on the lesson planning criteria. As with the first form described this rubric may be used regularly or periodically, and announced at the will of the instructor.

Rubric for Assessment of Case Analysis Process

Name: _____

Case #: _____

PARTICIPATION, FACILITATION, AND ATTITUDINAL ASPECTS

Use the following rating scale for your assessments: (high) 5, 4, 3.5, 3 (low)

	Self	Peer	Instructor	Total
1. Demonstrated *participation skills*, e.g., helped others, shared ideas, listened to others, refrained from distraction/annoying other, used appropriate humor, sought clarity, was prepared prior to group meeting	Rating: _____ Evidence: _____	Name 1: _____ Rating: _____ Evidence: _____ Name 2: _____ Rating: _____ Evidence: _____ Name 3: _____ Rating: _____ Evidence: _____	Rating: _____ Evidence: _____	_____
2. Employed *facilitation skills* when appropriate, e.g., suggested direction, provided encouragement, monitored time and group progress, helped facilitate decision making, generated new ways of viewing a simulation	Rating: _____ Evidence: _____	Name 1: _____ Rating: _____ Evidence: _____ Name 2: _____ Rating: _____ Evidence: _____ Name 3: _____ Rating: _____ Evidence: _____	Rating: _____ Evidence: _____	_____
3. Demonstrated *positive attitudes*, such as sensitivity to thoughts and feelings of others, thoughtfulness, commitment to task, honesty, integrity, and open-mindedness	Rating: _____ Evidence: _____	Name 1: _____ Rating: _____ Evidence: _____ Name 2: _____ Rating: _____ Evidence: _____ Name 3: _____ Rating: _____ Evidence: _____	Rating: _____ Evidence: _____	_____

Name: Rubric for Instructor Rating of Case Analysis Products

Criteria	5	4	3.5	3	Rating	Evidence
Identifies and addresses the important diversity issues embedded within the case	Diversity issues are identified and specifically addressed (e.g., race, class, gender, affectional orientation, age, etc.).	Diversity issues are identified but not specifically addressed.	Diversity issues are not identified or addressed.	Component not submitted.		
Acknowledges that there might be more than one view or perspective (i.e., multiple interpretations)	Multiple perspectives are acknowledged and these perspectives are thoroughly expressed within the case response.	Multiple perspectives are acknowledged, but the expressions of these perspectives are limited with the case response.	A single perspective is acknowledged and expressed.	Component not submitted.		
Reconciles differences in suggested conclusions, and derives preferred approach to the issue based on evidence cited	Identifies preferred approach and provides thorough evidence to support key assertions.	Provides limited evidence to support assertions.	Provides no evidence to support assertions.	Component not submitted.		
Presents responses (problems, evidence, conclusions, etc.) in a clear way	Case response is clearly articulated and is free of grammatical, usage, and mechanical errors.	Case response is articulated and a few grammatical, usage, or mechanical errors exist.	Case response is not clearly articulated, and grammatical, usage and mechanical errors impede comprehension.	Component not submitted.		
Relates key issues in the case to diversity-based: 1) lesson and unit planning, 2) instructional strategies, 3) student needs, 4) cultural backgrounds of students, 5) field experiences, and/or 6) professional standards in education	Key issues of the case are thoroughly related with best diversity-based instructional practices. The issues/practices alignment is clearly stated. Four out of the six practices are incorporated in the response.	Key issues of the case are somewhat related to best diversity-based, instructional practices. The issues/practices alignment is stated. Three out of the six practices are incorporated in the response.	Key issues of the case need to be identified and are not related to best diversity-based instructions/practices. The issues/practices alignment is not stated. Only one or two of the practices are incorporated in the response.	Component not submitted.		

Bibliography

General Education

Boykin, A. W. (1994). Afrocultural expression and its implications for schooling. In Hollins, E., King, J., and Hayman, W. (Eds.). *Teaching diverse populations: Formulating a knowledge base* (pp. 243–256). Albany, NY: Suny Press.

Covington, M. (1984). The self-worth theory of motivation. *Elementary School Journal, 85*(1), 5–20.

Danielson, C. (1996). *Enhancing professional practice: A framework for teaching.* Alexandria, VA: Association for Supervision and Curriculum Development.

Davis, L. (1996, April). Equality in education: An agenda for urban schools. *Equity & Excellence in Education,* 61–67.

Frey, D., & Carlock, C. J. (1989). *Enhancing self-esteem.* Muncie, IN: Accelerated Development.

Gage, N. L. (1978). *The scientific basis of the art of teaching.* New York: Perennial Library.

Glasser, W. (1985). *Control theory in the classroom.* New York: Teachers College Press.

Kolata, G., Laumann, E., Michael, R., & Gagnon, J. (1994). *Sex in America.* Chicago: National Opinion Research Center, University of Chicago.

Marzano, R. J. (1992). *A different kind of classroom: Teaching with dimensions of learning.* Alexandria, VA: Association for Supervision and Curriculum Development.

McNergney, R., Herbert, J., & Ford, R. (1994). Cooperation and competition in cases-based education. *Journal of Teacher Education, 45*(5), 339–345.

Redman, G. L. (1992). *Building self-esteem in students: A skill and strategy workbook for teachers.* 1480 Arden View Dr., Arden Hills, MN 55112.

Reed, S., & Sautter, R. (1990). Children of poverty—The status of 12 million young Americans. *Phi Delta Kappan, 71*(10), K1–K12.

Riley, S. S. (1984). *How to generate values in young children: Integrity, honesty, individuality, self-confidence, and wisdom.* Washington, DC: National Association for the Education of Young Children.

U.S. Department of Education. (1988). *Tenth annual report to Congress on the implementation of the handicapped act.* Washington, DC: Author.

Sources Containing Case Studies

Greenword, G. E., & Fillmer, H. T. (1997). *Professional core cases for teacher decision-making.* Upper Saddle River, NJ: Merrill/Prentice Hall.

Gorski, P. (2005). *Multicultural education and the Internet.* New York: Pearson Education.

Hinely, R., & Ford, K. (1995). *Education in Edge City: Cases for reflection and action.* Hillsdale, NJ: Lawrence Erlbaum.

Kaufman, J. M., Mostert, M. P., Nuttycombe, D. G., Trent, S. C., & Hallahan, D. P. (1993). *Managing classroom behavior: A reflective case-based approach.* Boston: Allyn & Bacon.

Kowalski, T. J., Weaver, R. A., & Henson, K. T. (1990). *Case studies on teaching.* New York: Longman.

Shulman, J. H., & Mesa-Bains, A. (Eds.). (1990). *Diversity in the classroom: A casebook for teachers and teacher education.* San Francisco: Research for Better Schools.

Silverman, R., Welty, W. M., & Lyons, S. (1994a). *Classroom assessment cases for teacher problem solving.* New York: McGraw-Hill.

Silverman, R., Welty, W. M., & Lyons, S. (1994b). *Classroom management cases for teacher problem solving.* New York: McGraw-Hill.

Silverman, R., Welty, W. M., & Lyons, S. (1994c). *Educational psychology cases for teacher problem solving.* New York: McGraw-Hill.

Silverman, R., Welty, W. M., & Lyons, S. (1994d). *Multicultural education cases for teacher problem solving.* New York: McGraw-Hill.

Silverman, R., Welty, W. M., & Lyons, S. (1994e). *Primis Education Series: Case studies for teacher problem solving.* New York: McGraw-Hill.

Silverman, R., Welty, W. M., & Lyons, S. (1996). *Case studies for teacher problem solving.* New York: McGraw-Hill.

Stipek, D. J. (1988). *Motivation to learn.* Upper Saddle River, NJ: Prentice Hall.

Wasserman, S. (1993). *Getting down to cases: Learning to teach with case studies.* New York: Teachers College Press.

Watson, C. R. (1997). *Middle school case studies.* Upper Saddle River, NJ: Merrill/Prentice Hall.

Reviews: Case Methods

Anderson, L. M., Blumenfeld, P., Pintrich, P. R., Clark, C. M., Marx, R. W., & Peterson, P. (1995). Educational psychology for teachers: Reforming our courses, rethinking our roles. *Educational Psychologist, 30*(3), 143–158.

Harrington, H., & Garrison, M. (1992). Cases as shared inquiry: A dialogical model of teacher preparation. *American Educational Research Journal, 29,* 715–735.

Merseth, K. (1996). Cases and case methods in teacher education. In J. Sikula (Ed.), *Handbook of research on teacher education* (pp. 722–746). New York: Macmillan/Simon & Schuster.

Empirical Studies: Case Methods

Levin, B. B. (1994). Using the case method in teacher education: The role of discussion and experience in teachers' thinking about cases. *Teacher and Teacher Education, 10*(2), 1–17.

Levin, B. B. (1996, April). *Learning from discussion: A comparison of computer-based versus face-to-face case discussions.* Paper presented at the American Educational Research Association Conference, New York.

Lundeberg, M. A. (1993). Case discussions in educational psychology. In V. Wolf (Ed.), *Improving the climate of the college classroom* (pp. 159–164). Madison, WI: University of Wisconsin System Office of Equal Opportunity Programs and Policy Studies.

Lundeberg, M. A., Coballes-Vega, C., Daly, K., Bowman, G., Uhren, P., & Greenberg, D. (1995). Wandering around the world: Building multicultural perspectives through K–12 telecommunications projects. *Journal of Technology and Teacher Education, 3*(4), 301–321.

Lundeberg, M. A., & Fawver, J. E. (1994). Thinking like a teacher: Encouraging cognitive growth in case analysis. *Journal of Teacher Education, 45*(4), 289–297.

Lundeberg, M. A., Matthew, D., & Scheurman, G. (1996, April). *Looking twice means seeing more: How knowledge affects case analysis.* Paper presented at the American Educational Research Association Conference, New York.

Case Methodology

Clandinin, D. J. (1992). Narrative and story in teacher education. In T. Russell & H. Munby (Eds.), *Teachers and teaching: From classroom to reflection.* Washington, DC: Falmer Press.

Cordeiro, P. (1998). Problem-based learning in educational administration: Enhancing learning transfer. *Journal of School Leadership, 8*(3), 280–302.

Dolmans, D., & Snellen-Balendong, H. (1997). Seven principles of effective case design for a problem-based curriculum. *Medical Teacher, 19*(3), 185–90.

Greenwood, G., & Parkay, F. W. (1989). *Case studies for teacher decision making.* New York: Random House.

Grossman, P. L. (1992). Teaching and learning with cases: Unanswered questions. In J. H. Shulman (Ed.), *Case methods in teacher education.* New York: Teachers College Press.

Hansen, A. (1997). Writing cases for teaching: Observations of a Practitioner. *Phi Delta Kappan, 78*(5), 398–404.

Huntchings, P. (1993). *Using cases to improve college teaching: A guide to more reflective practice.* Washington, DC: American Association for Higher Education.

Kagan, D. M., & Tippins, D. J. (1993). Classroom cases as gauges of professional growth. In M. O'Hair & S. Odell (Eds.), *Teacher Education Yearbook 1: Diversity and teaching* (pp. 98–110). New York: Harcourt Brace Jovanovich and the Association of Teacher Educators.

Merriam, S. B. (1998). *Qualitative research and case study applications in education.* San Francisco: Jossey-Bass.

Merseth, K. (1991). *The case for cases in teacher education.* Washington, DC: American Association for Higher Education.

Schon, D. A. (1983). *The reflective practitioner: How professions think in action.* New York: Basic Books.

Schon, D. A. (1991). *The reflective turn: Case studies in and on educational practice.* New York: Teachers College Press.

Schulman, J. H. (Ed.). (1992). *Case methods in teacher education.* New York: Teachers College Press.

Shulman, J. H., & Mesa-Bains, A. (Eds.). (1993). *Diversity in the classroom: A casebook for teachers and teacher educators.* Hillsdale, NJ: Research for Better Schools and Lawrence Erlbaum.

Sykes, G., & Bird, T. (1992). Teacher education and the case idea. In G. E. Grant (Ed.), *Review of research in education, Vol. 18.* Washington, DC: American Educational Research Association.

Tillman, B. (1995). Reflections on case method teaching. *Action in Teacher Education, XVII*(1), 1–8.

Journal Articles and Papers on Case Methods

Albanese, M., & Mitchell, S. (1993). Problem-based learning: A review of literature on its outcomes and implementation issues. *Academic Medicine, 68,* 52–81.

Carter, K. (1993). The place of story in research on teaching and teacher education. *Educational Researcher, 22*(1), 5–12.

Carter, K., & Gonzalez, L. (1993). Beginning teachers' knowledge of classroom events. *Journal of Teacher Education, 44,* 223–232.

Fourtner, A. W., Fourtner, C. R., & Herreid, C. F. (1994). Bad blood: A study of the Tuskegee syphilis project. *Journal of College Science Teaching, 23,* 277–285.

Harrington, H. L. (1994). Perspectives on cases. *International Journal of Qualitative Studies in Education, 7*(2), 117–133.

Harrington, H. L., & Garrison, J. (1992). Cases as shared inquiry: A dialogical model of teacher preparation. *American Educational Research Journal, 29*(4), 715–735.

Herreid, C. F. (1994). Case studies in science: A novel method of science education. *Journal of College Science Teaching, 23,* 221–229.

Kagan, D. M. (1993, Winter). Contexts for the use of classroom cases. *American Educational Research Journal, 30*(4), 703–723.

Kleinfeld, J. (1990a). Creating cases on your own. Fairbanks, AK: Department of Education, Rural College, University of Alaska.

Kleinfeld, J. (1990b). The special virtues of the case method in preparing teachers for minority schools. *Teacher Education Quarterly, 17*(1), 43–51.

Merseth, K. K., & Lacey, C. A. (1993). Weaving stronger fabric: The pedagogical promise of hypermedia and case methods in teacher education. *Teaching and Teacher Education, 9*(3), 283–299.

Sykes, G., & Bird, T. (1992). Teacher education and the case idea. *Review of Research in Education, 18,* 457–521.

Multiculturalism

Adams, M., Bell, L. A., & Griffin, P. (1997). *Teaching for diversity and social justice.* New York: Routledge.

Allen, R. (2005). Promoting diverse leadership: Shared cultural backgrounds can strengthen bridges. *Education Update, 47*(3), 1–3, 8.

Andrzejewski, J., & Alessio, J. (1999). *Education for global citizenship and social responsibility.* (Monograph). Burlington, VT: John Dewey Project on Progressive Education.

Banks, C. A. M. (2005). Improving multicultural education: *Lessons from the intergroup education movement.* New York: Teachers College Press.

Banks, C. A. M., & Banks, J. A. (1995). Equity pedagogy: An essential component of multicultural education. *Theory into practice, 34*(3), 152–158.

Banks, J. A. (1991). A curriculum for empowerment, action, and change. In C. E. Sleeter (Ed.), *Empowerment through multicultural education* (pp. 125–142). Albany, NY: State University of New York Press.

Banks, J. A. (1994a). *An introduction to multicultural education.* Boston: Allyn & Bacon.

Banks, J. A. (1994b). *Multiethnic education.* Boston: Allyn & Bacon.

Banks, J. A. (2005). *Multicultural education: Issues and perspectives* (5th ed.). New York: Wiley.

Banks, J. A. (2006). *Cultural diversity and education: Foundations, curriculum, and teaching.* Boston: Allyn & Bacon.

Banks, J. A., & Banks, C. A. M. (Eds.). (1997). *Multicultural education: Issues and perspectives.* Boston: Allyn & Bacon.

Banks, J. A., & Banks, C. A. M. (Eds.). (2004). *Handbook of research on multicultural education* (2nd ed.). San Francisco: Jossey-Bass.

Banks, J. A., Banks, C. A. M., Cortes, C. E., Hahn, C., Merryfield, M., Moodley, K. A., Murphy-Shigematsu, S., Osler, A., Park, C., & Parker, W. C. (2005). *Democracy and diversity: Principles and concepts for educating citizens in a global age.* Seattle, WA: Center for Multicultural Education, University of Washington.

Carey, K. (2004). The real value of teachers: Using new information about teacher effectiveness to close the achievement gap. *Thinking K–16: A Publication of the Education Trust, 8*(1), 3–42.

Chisholm, I. M. (1994). Culture and technology: Implications for multicultural teacher education. *Journal of Information Technology and Teacher Education, 3*(2), 213–228.

Christensen, L. (1994). Unlearning the myths that bind us. In B. Bigelow, L. Christensen, & J. Karp (Eds.), *Rethinking our classrooms: Teaching for equity and justice* (pp. 8–13). Milwaukee, WI: Rethinking Our Schools.

Christensen, R., & Karp, S. (Eds.). (2003). *Rethinking school reform: Views from the classroom.* Milwaukee, WI: Rethinking Our Schools.

Cochran-Smith, M. (1999). Learning to teach for social justice. In G. S. Griffin (Ed.), *The education of teachers: Ninety-eighth yearbook of the national society for the study of education* (pp. 114–144). Chicago: The University of Chicago Press.

Cox, S. S.-K. (2003). International adoption of mixed race children. In M. P. P. Root & M. Kelle (Eds.), *Multiracial child resource book: Living complex identities* (pp. 116–123). Seattle, WA: Mavin Foundation.

Darder, A. (1991). *Culture and power in the classroom.* New York: Bergin and Garvey.

Derman-Sparks, L., Phillips, C. B., & Hilliard III, A. G. (1997). *Teaching/learning anti-racism: A developmental approach.* New York: Teachers College Press.

Dilg, M. (2003). *Thriving in the multicultural classroom: Principles and practices for effective teaching.* New York: Teachers College Press.

Gaff, J. G. (1992). Beyond politics: The educational issues inherent in multicultural education. *Change, 24*(1), 31–35.

Garcia, E. (2004). Educating Mexican American students: Past treatment and recent developments in theory, research, policy, and practice. In J. A. Banks & C. A. M. Banks (Eds.), *Handbook of research on multicultural education* (2nd ed., pp. 491–514). San Francisco: Jossey-Bass.

Gay, G. (1994). *At the essence of learning: Multicultural education.* West Lafayette, IN: Kappa Delta Pi.

Gay, G. (2000). *Culturally responsive teaching: Theory, research, and practice.* New York: Teachers College Press.

Gay, G. (2005). Educational equality for students of color. In J. A. Banks & C. A. M. Banks (Eds.), *Multicultural education: Issues and perspectives* (5th ed., pp. 211–241). Hoboken, NJ: Wiley.

Gay, G. (2005). Politics of multicultural teacher education. *Journal of Teacher Education, 56*(10), 221–228.

Gillborn, D., & Ladson-Billings, G. (Eds.). (2004). *The Routledge Falmer multicultural education reader.* New York: RoutledgeFalmer.

Gollnick, D. M. & Chinn, P. C. (2002). *Multicultural education in a pluralistic society* (6th ed.). Upper Saddle River: Merrill/Prentice Hall.

Gorski, P. (2005). *Multicultural education and the Internet: Internations and integrations* (2nd ed.). New York: McGrawHill.

Grant, C. A., & Gomez, M. L. (Eds.). (1996). *Making schooling multicultural: Campus and classroom.* Upper Saddle River, NJ: Merrill/Prentice Hall.

Grant, C. A., & Sleeter, C. E. (1998). *Turning on learning.* Upper Saddle River, NJ: Merrill/Prentice Hall.

Green, R. L. (2005). *Expectations: How teacher expectations can increase student achievement and assist in closing the achievement gap.* Columbus, OH: SRA/McGraw-Hill.

Guthrie. J. W. (Ed.). (2003). *No Child Left Behind Act of 2001. Encyclopedia of Education* (2nd ed., Vol. 8, pp. 3087–3090). New York: Macmillan Reference U.S.A.

Harris, I. M., & Morrison, M. L. (2003). *Peace education* (2nd ed.). Jefferson, NC: McFarland.

Helms, J. (Ed.). (1990). *Black and white racial identity: Theory, research, and practice.* Westport, CT: Praeger.

Higgins, J. J. (2003). *Multicultural children's literature: Creating and applying an evaluation tool in response to the needs of urban educators.* New Horizons for Learning. Retrieved from http://www.newhorizons.org/startegies/multicultural/higgis.htm

Hittleman, D. (1978). *Developmental reading: A psycholinguistic perspective.* Chicago: Rand-McNally.

Irvine, J. I. (2003). *Educating teachers for diversity: Seeing with a cultural eye.* New York: Teachers College Press.

Jennings, T. (1994). Self in connection as a component of human-rights advocacy. *The Journal of Moral Education, 23*(3), 285–295.

King, J. L. (2004). Culture-centered knowledge: Black studies, curriculum transformation, and social action. In J. A. Banks & C. A. M. Banks (Eds.), *Handbook of research on multicultural education* (2nd ed., pp. 349–378). San Francisco: Jossey-Bass.

Kosmin, B. A. (1991). *Highlights of the CJF 1990 national Jewish population survey.* New York: Council of the Jewish Federation, pp. 3–6, 10, 20–22, 25–26. Reprinted in Feagin, J., & Feagin, C. (1993). Racial and ethnic relations (4th ed.). Upper Saddle River, NJ: Prentice Hall.

Ladson-Billings, G. (2005). Is the team all right? Diversity and teacher education. *Journal of Teacher Education, 56*(10), 229–234.

Leonhardt, D. (2004, August 27). More Americans were uninsured and poor in 2003, census finds. *New York Times,* p. A18.

Levine, A., & Cureton, J. (1992). The quiet revolution: Eleven facts about multiculturalism and the curriculum. *Change, 24*(1), 25–29.

Litchner, J. H., & Johnson, D. (1973). Changes in attitudes toward Negroes by White elementary students after the use of multiethnic readers. *Journal of Educational Psychology, 65*, 295–299.

Lomawaima, K. T. (2004). Educating Native Americans. In J. A. Banks & C. A. M. Banks (Eds.), *Handbook of research on multicultural education* (2nd ed., pp. 441–461). San Francisco: Jossey-Bass.

Lu, M. Y. (1998). *Multicultural children's literature in the elementary classroom.* Bloomington, IN: ERIC Clearinghouse on Reading English and Communication. (ERIC Document Reproduction Service No. ED423552)

Luchtenberg, S. (Ed.). (2004). *Migration, education, and change.* New York: Routledge.

McAdams, Donald R. (2000). *Fighting to save our urban schools . . . and winning!: Lessons from Houston.* New York: Teachers College Press.

Merryfield, M., & Wilson, A. (2005). *Global perspectives in the Social Studies.* Silver Spring, MD: National Council for the Social Studies.

Minami, M., & Ovando, C. J. (2004). Language issues in multicultural contexts. In J. A. Banks & C. A. M. Banks (Eds.), *Handbook of research on multicultural education* (2nd ed., pp. 567–588). San Francisco: Jossey-Bass.

Moll, A. (2005). *Differentiated instruction guide for inclusive teaching* (p. 4). New York: Dude Publishing.

Moll, I. C., & Gonzalez, N. (2004). Engaging life: A funds-of-knowledge approach to multicultural education. In J. A. Banks & C. A. M. Banks (Eds.), *Handbook of research on multicultural education* (2nd ed., pp. 736–750). San Francisco: Jossey-Bass.

NAME Standards Committee. (2002). *Criteria for evaluatinq state curriculum standards* (Draft).

National Collaborative on Diversity in the Teaching Force. (2004). *Assessment of diversity in America's teaching force.* Washington, DC: National Education Association.

National Commission on Terrorist Attacks upon the United States. (2004). *The 9/11 Commission report.* New York: Norton.

Nieto, S. (1999). *The light in their eyes: Creating multicultural learning communities.* New York: Teachers College Press.

Nieto, S. (2000). *Affirming diversity: The sociopolitical context of multicultural education* (3rd ed.). Reading, MA: Longman.

Nilsen, A. P., & Donelson, K. L. (2001). *Literature for today's young adults* (6th ed.). New York: Longman.

Noguera, P. (2003). *City schools and the American dream: Reclaiming the promise of public education.* New York: Teachers College Press.

Noguera, P. A. (2003). The trouble with Black boys: The role and influence of environmental and cultural factors on the academic performance of African American males. *Urban Education, 38,* 431–459.

Norton, D. E. (1983). *Through the eyes of a child.* Columbus, OH: Merrill.

Oakes, L., Joseph, R., & Muir, K. (2004). Access and achievement in mathematics and science: Inequalities that endure and change. In J. A. Banks & C. A. M. Banks (Eds.), *Handbook of research on multicultural education* (2nd ed., pp. 699–715). San Francisco: Jossey-Bass.

Obidah, J., & Howard, T. (2005). Preparing teachers for 'Monday morning' in the urban school classroom: Reflectioning on our pedagogies and practices as effective teacher educators. *Journal of Teacher Education, 56*(3), 248–255.

Pang, V. O., Kiang, P. N., & Pak, Y. K. (2004). Asian Pacific Americans: Challenging a biased educational system. In J. A. Banks & C. A. M. Banks (Eds.), *Handbook of research on multicultural education* (2nd ed., pp. 542–563). San Francisco: Jossey-Bass.

Perry, T., & Delpit (Eds.). (1998). The real ebonics debate: Power, language and the education of African-American Children. Boston: Beacon Press.

Phelan, P., Davidson, A. L., & Yu, H. C. (1993). Students' multiple worlds: Navigating the borders of family, peer and school cultures. In A. L. Davidson & P. Phelan (Eds.), *Renegotiating cultural diversity in American schools* (pp. 52–88). New York: Teachers College Press.

Pusch, M. D. (1979). *Multicultural education: A cross-cultural training approach.* Yarmouth, ME: International Press.

Rasinski, T. V., & Padak, N. D. (1990). Multicultural learning through children's literature. *Language Arts, 67,* 576–580.

Reyes, P., Scribner, J. D., & Scribner, A. P. (Eds.). (1999). *Lessons from high performing Hispanic schools: Creating learning communities.* New York: Teachers College Press.

Root, M. P. P., & Kelley, M. (Eds.). (2004). *Multicultural child resource book.* Seattle, WA: Mavin Foundation.

Rose, S. J. (2000). *Social stratification in the United States.* New York: New Press.

Sadar, Z., & David, M. (2004). *Islam.* London: Verso.

Sheets, R. H. (2005). Diversity pedagogy: Examining the rate of culture in the teaching-learning process. Boston: Allyn and Bacon.

Sleeter, C. (2001). Preparing teachers for culturally diverse schools: Research and the overwhelming presence of Whiteness. *Journal of Teacher Education, 52*(2), 94–106.

Sleeter, C. E., & McLaren, P. L. (Eds.). (1995). *Multicultural education, critical pedagogy, and the politics of difference.* Albany, NY: State University of New York Press.

Spindler, G., & Spindler, L. (Eds.). (1994). *Pathways to cultural awareness: Cultural therapy with teachers and students.* Thousand Oaks, CA: Sage.

Stephan, W. G., & Vogt, W. P. (Eds.). (2004). *Education programs for improving intergroup relations: Theory, research, and practice.* New York: Teachers College Press.

Stevens, R. (2003). *Listening to students' voices: Evaluating students' learning, hearing professors' voices: The debate about teacher education.* Conference presentation at the meeting of the American Association of Colleges for Teacher Education, New Orleans, LA.

Suarez-Orozco, M. M., & Paez, M. M. (Eds.). (2002). *Latinos remaking America.* Berkeley, CA: University of California Press.

Tatum, B. D. (1992). Talking about race, learning about racism: The application of racial identity development theory in the classroom. *Harvard Education Review, 62*(1), 1–24.

Teaching tolerance. Available from Teaching Tolerance, Order Department, 400 Washington Avenue, Montgomery, AL 36104.

Tiedt, P., & Tiedt, I. (2006). Multicultural teaching: A handbook of activities, information, and resources, 7/e, Boston: Allyn and Bacon.

Trudgill, P. (1984). *Sociolinguistics: An introduction to language and society.* New York: Penguin.

Tutwiler, S. J. Winn. (2005). Teachers as collaborative partners: Working with diverse families and communities. Mahwah, New Jersey: Lawrence Erlbaum Associates, Publishers.

Understanding Islam and the Muslims. (1989). Washington, DC: The Embassy of Saudi Arabia. Reprinted in Bennett, C. (1995). Comprehensive multicultural education theory and practice. Needham Heights, MA: Allyn & Bacon.

UNESCO. (2004). *Shared values, cultural diversity and education: What to learn and how.* Case study for the International conference on Education. Retrieved on March 8, 2004, from www.ibe.unesco.org/International/ICE/pdf/pdfbg3e.pdf

United for a Fair Economy. (2004). *Distribution of U.S. wealth ownership in 2001.* Retrieved March 16, 2005, from http://www.faireconomy.org/research/wealth_charts:html

U.S. Census Bureau. (2001). *Statistical abstract of the United States: 2000* (120th ed.). Washington, DC: U.S. Government Printing Office.

U.S. Census Bureau. (2003). *Statistical abstract of the United States: 2003* (123th ed.). Washington, DC: U.S. Government Printing Office.

Villegas, A. M., & Lucas, T. (2002). Preparing culturally responsive teachers. *Journal of Teacher Education, 53*(1), 20–32.

Vinson, K., Gibson, R., & Ross, E. W. (2001). *High-stakes testing and standardization: The threat to authenticity.* Monograph in *Progressive Perspectives,* University of Vermont: John Dewey Project on Progressive Education.

Internet Resources

General Educational Resources

Edweb	http://www.edwebproject.org
ERIC	http://ericir.syr.edu (lesson plans, databases, and so on)
Internet Public Library	http://www.ipl.org/ref

| Kathy Schrock's Guide | http://www.capecod.net//Schrockguide |
| U.S. Department of Education | http://www.ed.gov/lVlib. |

Teaching with Technology

T.H.E. Online	http://www.thejournal.com (Journal of Technology in Higher Education)
Teaching with Technology	http://www.uvm.edu/jmorris
Web 66	http://web66.coled.umn.edu (to set-up webservers)

Classroom Resources for Equity and Social Justice

| Rethinking Schools | http://www.rethinkingschools.org |

Listservs and Newsgroups

| Multicultural Education | E-mail:MULTCED@umddumd.edu
http//www.wmht.org/trail/explor02 |
| Teacher Training and Multiculturalism | http://unesco.uneb.edu/educnews/multiculturalism
http://www.valdosta.peachnet.edu/~whuitt/educ. html#mc |

Glossary

Chapter 2

critical thinking

> Higher-level thinking (analytical, careful judgment, synthesis) such as carefully judging the merit or truth of text material.

discrimination

> The denial of fair treatment and justice by individuals and institutions in areas, such as education, housing, employment, banking, and political rights; actions that often follow prejudicial thought.

gender equity (gender fair)

> Fair, just, impartial treatment of males and females within a society and its institutions.

prejudice

> A preconceived attitude or opinion formed without sufficient knowledge; frequently based on stereotypes; usually unfavorable but can be favorable in intent (although even "favorable" prejudices have the unfavorable effect of categorizing individuals or groups).

reinforcement (of learning and/or behavior)

> Encouraging or rewarding; strengthening.

relevant curriculum

> Curriculum that has meaning because it connects with the prior knowledge and experience of the learner.

sexism

> Unfair or inequitable treatment of persons because of their gender.
> Economic, political, and social structures that give one sex group an advantage over the other. Stereotypes and misinformation about the biological characteristics of each sex group reinforce discrimination. Historically, in most societies, women have been victimized; however, males are also victimized by sexist beliefs and practices.

social-emotional classroom climate

> Feeling tones experienced by students within a classroom, e.g., warmth, acceptance, affection, distance, intimidation, confusion, frustration.

teacher flexibility and responsiveness

> The degree to which a teacher is flexible in terms of curriculum and instruction and is responsive to student needs and interests.

teacher–student interaction patterns

> The quantity and quality of verbal and nonverbal communication that goes on between teacher and students. Such patterns can either build or denigrate student self-esteem and can either warm or cool the social-emotional classroom climate.

traditional social and role concepts

> Social status and roles historically assigned to males and females, e.g., for males—masculine/athletic, independent, breadwinner; for females—feminine, nurturant, dependent.

wait time

> The amount of time a teacher waits after posing a question, before rephrasing, answering it, giving a cue, or making another comment. (Recommended wait time is at least three to five seconds for most simple questions; longer for those that require more complex thinking, e.g., analysis, synthesis, evaluation.)

Chapter 3

cultural competence

> Culturally relevant teaching often associated with positive perspectives of parents and families, communication of high expectations, learning within the context of culture, student-centered instruction, reshaping the curriculum, and teachers as facilitator. (Gay, 2000)

cultural norms

> Widespread practices or customs characteristic of a particular culture.

culture

> The sum total of ways of living, including values, beliefs, aesthetic standards, linguistic expression, patterns of thinking, behavioral norms, and styles of communication that a group of people has developed to assure its survival in a particular physical and human environment. (Pusch, 1979)

democracy in the classroom

> The degree to which students are empowered to participate in decision making (e.g., regarding classroom rules or procedures).

ethnic group

> A social construct that divides people into social groups based on characteristics such as shared sense of group membership, history, ancestral geographic base, language, political and economic interests, behavioral patterns and values. Examples of ethnic groups are: Haitian & African American (Black); Cherokee & Navajo (Native American); Polish, Irish, & French (White); Chinese, Korean, & Vietnamese (Asian); Cuban, Mexican, & Puerto Rican (Latino). (Adams, Bell, & Griffin, 1997)

ethnocentrism

> Pride in and focus on one's own ethnicity. If overextended, can lead to feeling of superiority and to discrimination against people of different ethnicities.

interdisciplinary teaching

> Teaching based on demonstrating connections between and among two or more disciplines (subject matter areas).

learning styles (cultural)

> Learning preferences linked to the cultural ethos of a group of people, e.g., stylistic behaviors of many African Americans such as: a preference for oral modalities of communication, an emphasis on affect/emotions, a spiritual rather than a mechanistic view of life, expressiveness emphasizing movement, rhythm, music, and dance, among others. (Boykin, 1994)

multiculturalism

> A philosophical view, a movement/approach that includes and honors the history, heritage, culture, and contributions of gender, racial, ethnic, linguistic, religious, economic, special needs, sexual orientation, and other groups in curriculum, instruction, and the total school environment.

rule consequence

> The result of following or violating a classroom rule or procedure, e.g., privileges restitution, time-out, dismissal from class, and the like.

social justice curriculum

> Curriculum that in content and process provides equal access to and equal outcomes for all students; that seeks excellence and equity; that actively seeks to eliminate preexisting social, political, and economic inequities.

stereotype

> An overgeneralized, often negative view of an entire population or group of people without regard for their individual differences. While some stereotypes may be meant to be complimentary, even they are hurtful in that they categorize people without regard for individuality.

Chapter 4

access

> A barrier-free opportunity to learn and use materials, resources, and events in natural settings. (Moll, 2005)

agent group

> A group which often targets another group or groups for discrimination. In U.S.A. society, White males are normally considered positioned to be this agent group.

classism

> Prejudice and/or discrimination against people because of their real or perceived economic status.

equity pedagogy

> Teaching that facilitates the academic achievement of students from diverse racial, cultural, gender, and social-class groups. (Banks & Banks, 1995)

experiential knowledge

> Knowledge or practical wisdom gained from what one has observed, encountered, or undergone.

institutional racism

> The network of institutional structures, policies, and practices that create advantages and benefits for agent groups (e.g. Whites), and discrimination, oppression, and disadvantages for people from targeted groups. The advantages created for Whites are often invisible to them, or are considered "rights" available to everyone as opposed to "privileges" awarded only to some. (Adams, Bell, & Griffin, 1997)

knowledge base

> Research-derived knowledge upon which a discipline (e.g., sociology, teacher education, or psychology) is built.

oppression

> A state of deprivation of human rights or privilege; persecution of a group of people by another with the power to make and enforce laws on a broad scale.

power

> The ability to make and enforce laws that affect a large group of people (e.g., a state or nation) over a period of time.

race as a socially constructed concept

> Categories based on perceived physical differences between and among human groups; a social construct that arbitrarily divides people on characteristics such as skin color, facial form, or eye shape, ancestral history, heritage, and culture, and the social, political, and economic needs of a society at a particular period of time.

racism

> Prejudice or discrimination toward persons because of their race.

social action activities

> Activities that encourage students to think about and take action with the purpose of creating a more fair or just condition, e.g., eliminating some form of injustice or oppression in a classroom, school, or community.

student self-esteem

> A student's feeling of being lovable and capable; a student's assessment of his or her own value or worth.

target group

> A group of people who are targeted for bias or discrimination, e.g., persons of color, GLBT orientation, etc.

tracking

> The placement of students in classroom or program based on ability, i.e., homogeneous grouping. Generally thought to have detrimental effects on the psychological and academic growth of all students, especially of those in tracks other than the "highest" track. Common tracks include the college track, vocational track and remedial track.

White privilege

> The concrete benefits of access to resources and social rewards and the power to shape the norms and values of society that Whites receive, unconsciously or consciously, by virtue of their skin color in a racist society. (Adams, Bell, & Griffin, 1997)

Chapter 5

assessment criteria

> Standards used to assess the degree to which a goal has been attained.

behavior modification

> The direct altering of unwanted behaviors by means of reinforcement, ignoring, and/or punishment (conditioning), or biofeedback.

effects of childrearing practices

> Emotional/psychological/physical effects of a given approach to parenting in general, or behavior management more specifically.

emotional literacy

> Awareness of knowledge and dispositions related to self and how one relates to others; level of self-awareness and understanding of own thoughts and feelings.

establishing incentives

> The process of setting up positive consequences of specified behavior, e.g., a reward; a desired (motivating) outcome of completing a task.

free and reduced-price lunch programs

> Programs designed to serve meals in schools with high proportions of students of poverty.

high-poverty school

A school with a high proportion of students of poverty.

poverty

As measured by the government on the basis of income, a family of three with an income of less than $13,314 per year. (Rose, 2000)

S.E.S.

The socioeconomic status of a person or group.

Chapter 6

anti-Semitism

Prejudice and/or discrimination against Jews; can be based on hatred of Jews because of their ethnicity, religious beliefs, or the erroneous belief that Jews are a race.

Islam

The term Islam means peace. The Islam religion creed consists of a two-part statement: "There is no god but God; and Prophet Muhammad is the messenger of God." Anyone who makes this declaration—known as the shahadah, meaning bearing witness—freely and sincerely is a Muslim. Muhammad is a model of love, gentleness, fairness, equality and brotherhood. (Sardar & Davies, 2004)

Judaism

A monotheistic religion based on the Holy Scripture and the Talmud; provides the historical basis of both Protestantism and Catholicism.

provisions of the First Amendment to the Constitution

Practices allowed and not allowed by the First Amendment to the U.S. Constitution.

religious symbols

Emblem, sign, or representation of a religion.

separation of school and state

The requirement that religion (or absence of) not be promoted or demoted by the public schools.

spirituality

Belief in a life-giving force; for some, presence of God; related to sacred or religious matters.

values

Deeply held beliefs that have been chosen freely from alternatives, and are cherished and acted on over time. A belief or attitude that is highly treasured and that guides behavior.

Chapter 7

ableism

> Prejudicial attitudes and discriminatory actions directed against people with disabilities.

accommodation

> A modification of curriculum or instruction to more effectively meet the needs of students, especially special needs students.

culturally and linguistically diverse (CLD)

> Students with a cultural background and a language that is different from that of dominant society.

disability

> A physical, mental, or sensory condition that interferes with a person's ability to do something, e.g., learn, walk, see, hear. Preferred usage is as a descriptive noun and adjective, as in "person with disabilities."

grouping strategies

> Various ways of organizing students into groups for the purpose of learning.

Individualized Education Program (IEP)

> A program designed specifically to meet the needs of a particular student, especially a student with a special need, e.g., a visual or hearing impaired student.

Individuals with Disabilities Education Act (IDEA)

> Provides for a free appropriate public education for all students with disabilities, in the least restrictive environment.

Individuals with Disabilities Education Improvement Act (2004) (IDEIA)

> Aligns with the No Child Left Behind Act and focuses outcomes for students with disabilities rather than on the special education process; also emphasizes the need to reduce paperwork and expand possibilities for reducing disagreements between schools and parents. It became effective July 1, 2005.

learning disabled

> Any condition characterized in school-age children by difficulty in accomplishing specific tasks, especially reading and writing, and associated with impaired development of a part of the central nervous system.

Chapter 8

bisexual

> A male or female who is attracted sexually and emotionally to both males and females.

family

"Two or more persons who share resources, responsibilities for decisions, values, and goals, and have commitments to one another over a period of time. The family is that climate that one comes home to; and it is that network of sharing and commitments that most accurately describes the family unit, regardless of blood, or adoption, or marriage." (American Home Economics Association)

gay

A generic term that applies to both men and women who are attracted to another of the same sex. Some people object to the use of gay when applied to lesbians as well as gay men, and use the word only to mean a homosexual male. The word has its origins in the 13th century meaning "merry," associated with troubadours who sang of courtly, and sometimes same-sex, love.

gender dysphoria

A psychological term used to describe the feelings of pain and anguish that arise from a transgender person's conflict between his or her gender identity (internal experience) and his or her biological sex (external experience).

GLBT

This acronym for gay/lesbian/bisexual/transgender is an umbrella term that covers both sexual orientation and gender identification. Other variations include LGBT, LGBTA (allies), GLBTI (intersex) and LGBTQ (questioning/queer).

heterosexism

The institutionalized assumption that everyone is heterosexual and that heterosexuality or bisexuality is the exception. This institution is maintained by pervasive images of heterosexuals in the media and also by the assumption that everyone is heterosexual. These images and assumptions allow straight people the privilege to not have to "come out."

heterosexual

Someone who forms sexual and affectionate relationships with members of the other gender. Also referred to as "straight."

heterosexual privilege

The basic civil rights and social privileges that a heterosexual individual automatically receives, which are systematically denied to gay, lesbian, or bisexual persons on the sole basis of their sexual orientation (e.g., marriage, hospital visitation rights, holding hands without fear of repercussion).

homophobia

The irrational fear of, hatred of, aversion to, or discrimination against homosexuals or homosexual behaviors. Homophobia consists of three separate components: sexism, xenophobia (fear of difference), and erotophobia (fear of sexual desire). "Biphobia" and "transphobia" are more specific terms when discussing prejudice toward bisexual and transgender persons, respectively.

homosexual

A man or woman who is attracted sexually/erotically and emotionally to persons of the same sex. Most gay, lesbian, and bisexual people today do not like to use this term to define themselves because of the word's history of use to anthologize and medicalize same-sex behavior.

inclusive language

The use of gender nonspecific language (e.g., "partner" instead of "husband") to avoid heterosexist assumptions.

internalized homophobia

The experience of shame, aversion, or self-hatred in reaction to one's own feelings of attraction for a person of the same sex.

intersexed individuals

People born with a combination of male and female characteristics of the reproductive and sexual systems. These characteristics may be noticeable immediately at birth or sometimes not until the onset of puberty. Intersexed individuals were formally known as hermaphrodites, although this term is now considered offensive. It was formerly believed that intersexed individuals needed to be placed firmly into one sex via surgery and/or hormones at the onset of visible intersexed characteristic. Many times these treatments were administered without regard to the individual's desires. This treatment is now considered malpractice, and organizations, such as the Intersex Society of North America, exist to provide public education and support for intersexed individuals.

lesbian

Used as an adjective or noun in reference to a female who has a same-sex orientation, i.e., attraction to another of the same gender.

LGBT

Abbreviations for lesbian, gay, bisexual, transgender persons; many prefer it to the older GLBT, which placed men in the traditional first place.

out

To be open about one's sexual orientation or gender identity.

partner or significant other

Primary domestic partner or spousal relationship(s). May refer to "girlfriend/ boyfriend," "lover," "roommate," "life partner," "wife/husband" or other terms.

pink triangle

A popular symbol for the GLBT rights movement. The symbol was originally used in Nazi Germany death camps, when homosexual prisoners were forced to wear pink inverted triangles.

queer

Used by some within the GLBT community to refer to a person who is gay, lesbian, bisexual, or transgender, or someone who is supportive of GLBT issues. This term is often as much a political statement as a label. Those who use the term feel it is more inclusive, allowing for the variety in race, class, ability, age, and gender that is present in GLBT communities. Others are offended by this word and view it as a pejorative.

questioning

A term or label used to identify those who are exploring personal issues of sexual orientation and/or gender identity.

sexual orientation

The inclination or capacity to develop intimate emotional and sexual relationships with people of the same gender, the other gender, or either gender. One's sexual orientation, therefore, may be heterosexual, homosexual, bisexual, or asexual.

transgender

A broad umbrella term used to describe the continuum of individuals whose gender identity and expression does not correspond with their genetic sex, e.g., transexuals and transvestites (male or female impersonators). Some transgender persons wish to change their self-perception; others have no such desire. There is no correlation between sexual orientation and gender identity; transgender persons can be heterosexual, gay, lesbian, or bisexual. Some people abbreviate the term "trans" or even "T."

transsexual

An individual who presents him/herself and lives as the genetic "opposite" to his/her genetic gender at birth. Most transsexuals alter, or would like to alter, their bodies through hormonal therapy, sex reassignment surgery (SRS), or other means. Transsexualism is sometimes divided into two stages: primary transsexualism (emerging in childhood) and secondary transsexualism (emerging during or after puberty).

transvestite

The original term for cross-dressing for emotional comfort or erotic fulfillment. Some today consider this term pejorative.

xenophobia

Fear of difference, actual or perceived.

Chapter 9

bilingual

> Ability to use two languages.

bilingual programs

> Educational programs that involve the use of two languages in instruction. Various forms include but are not limited to: immersion in students' second language for a year or two before switching to their first language as the medium for learning, and a traditional approach in which students receive content instruction in their first language while learning English as their second (or third, etc.) language.

Black English vernacular/Ebonics

> Also called African American English/African American Language, this term refers to the language system characteristically spoken in African American communities. For an in-depth discussion of the controversy surrounding the use of Ebonics in teaching, see Perry and Delpit, 1998.

Culturally and linguistically diverse (CLD)

> Persons who are of a culture different from the dominant mainstream culture of the country in which they live (e.g., the U.S.A.) and who speak a language other than the native language (e.g., English, in the U.S.A.) spoken in the country in which they live.

English language learners (ELL)

> Students who are in the process of learning English (and who may speak one or several other languages).

English as a second language (ESL)

> An educational approach to teaching English to students who have another native/first language. While ESL programs are often essential to regular education programs, they can also stand alone.

limited English proficiency (LEP)

> Usually refers to a student whose primary language is other than that of English, and who has limited knowledge and skill in speaking English.

low-incidence population

> Groups of speakers of a language other than English too small to have legal access to a bilingual program—in most states, typically less than 20 students.

Chapter 10

aged

> Persons who have matured into their mid-60s and above.

ageism

> Prejudice and/or discrimination towards members of a certain age group, e.g., teens, senior citizens.

bullying

Intimidation or hurting of usually a smaller, weaker, person; can be emotional or physical in nature.

child abuse

Emotional, psychological, physical, or sexual mistreatment of children; also neglect of children.

cyberbullying

harrassment utilizing technology including instant messaging, cell phone text messaging, online gaming, chat rooms, blogs (online journals), and social networking websites. Sometimes referred to as e-bullying.

elderly

Persons past middle age; labels vary but usually refers to persons in their 70s and above.

harassment

Persistent disturbance, tormenting, attack; emotional, physical, or sexual are common forms.

stages of development

A school of thought that acknowledges that growth occurs in predictable stages, e.g., stages of moral reasoning, racial identity, cognitive ability, and the like; often related to but not synonymous with age.

youth-oriented culture

A culture in which norms, traditions, conventions, promote and/or value youth; media depictions of those of youthful age as more glamorous, and generally of greater value.